John
Celebrates
the
Gospel

Ernest W. Saunders

John Celebrates the Gospel

📖 Abingdon Press
Nashville and New York

JOHN CELEBRATES THE GOSPEL

Originally published as COMING TO LIFE: A STUDY OF THE GOSPEL OF JOHN

Copyright © 1968 by Ernest W. Saunders

All rights in this book are reserved.
No part of the book may be reproduced in any manner whatsoever without written permission of the publishers except brief quotations embodied in critical articles or reviews. For information address Abingdon Press, Nashville, Tenenssee.

Standard Book Number: 687-20306-6

Library of Congress Catalog Card Number: 68-23404

Scripture quotations are from the Revised Standard Version of the Bible, copyrighted 1946 and 1952 by the Division of Christian Education, National Council of Churches, and are used by permission. In a few passages the translation is that of the New English Bible, New Testament, © the Delegates of the Oxford University Press and the Syndics of the Cambridge University Press; reprinted by permission.

PRINTED AND BOUND BY THE
PARTHENON PRESS AT NASHVILLE,
TENNESSEE, UNITED STATES OF AMERICA

For Verina

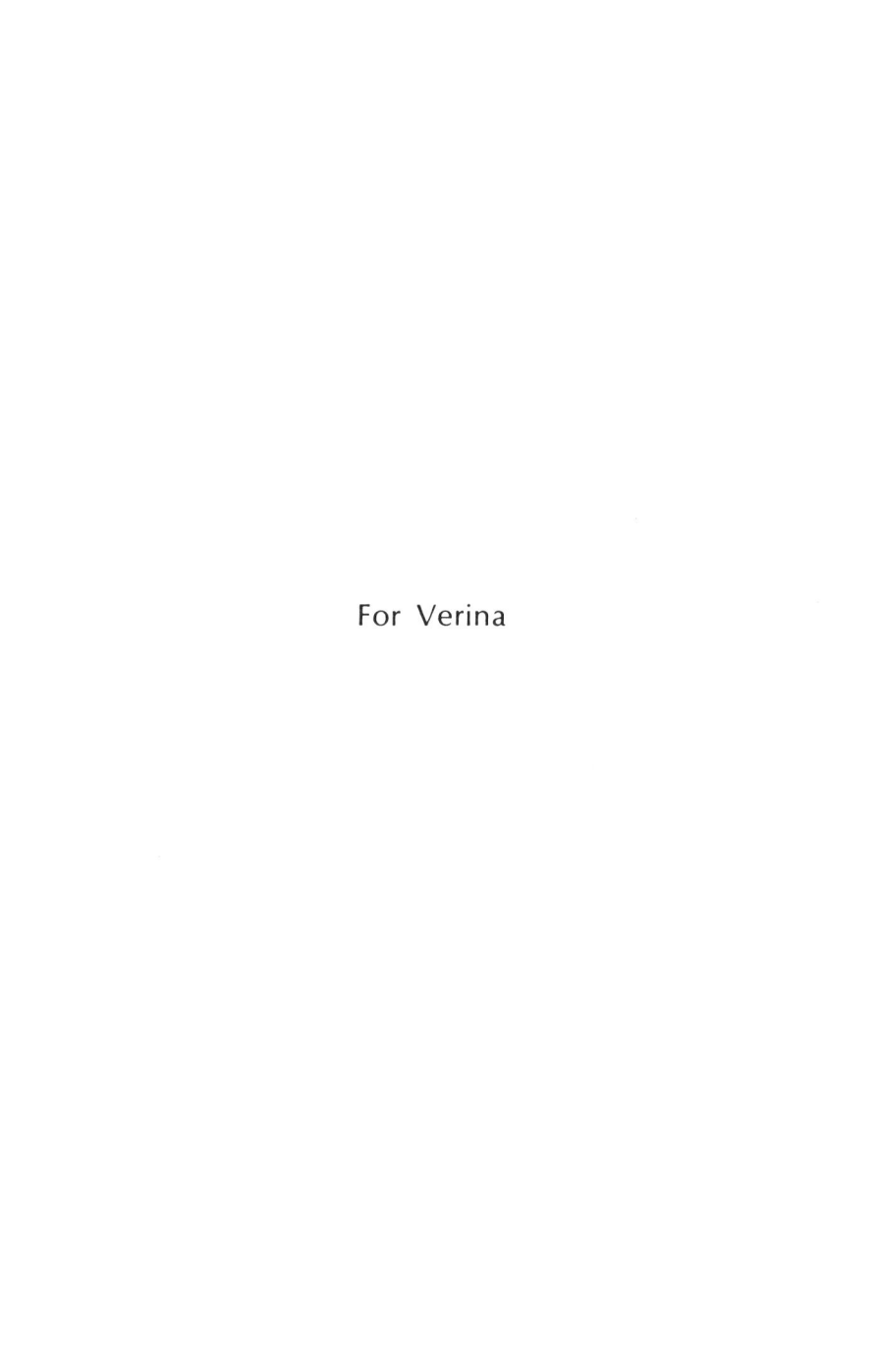

Contents

FOREWORD		ix
SELECTION FROM FAUST: A TRAGEDY BY GOETHE		x
CHAPTER I:	WHY ANOTHER GOSPEL?	1
CHAPTER II:	WHAT'S THE GOOD WORD?	27
	◆ 1:1 - 18 ◆	
CHAPTER III:	THE WORD IN THE WORLD	53
	◆ 1:19 - 6:71 ◆	
CHAPTER IV:	COMING TO LIFE	85
	◆ 7:1 - 12:50 ◆	
CHAPTER V:	DYING TO LIVE	111
	◆ 13:1 - 17:26 ◆	
CHAPTER VI:	THE LORD OF LIFE AND DEATH	141
	◆ 18:1 - 21:25 ◆	
"LET YOUR SPIRIT BREAK IN"		165
NOTES FOR CHAPTER I		166
NOTES FOR CHAPTER II		167
NOTES FOR CHAPTER III		169
NOTES FOR CHAPTER IV		172
NOTES FOR CHAPTER V		173
NOTES FOR CHAPTER VI		175
GLOSSARY		177
BOOKS SUGGESTED FOR FURTHER READING		184

Foreword

GRATEFUL ACKNOWLEDGEMENT is made of the courtesy extended by Prentice-Hall, Inc. for permission to quote several lines from the final chapter of my book, *Jesus In The Gospels*. Some of the interpretations appearing on the following pages found earlier form in a series of lessons on "John—Gospel of Eternal Life" and also appear in the 1968 issue of *The International Lesson Annual*, edited by Horace R. Weaver. My principal debt, however, is owed to students at Garrett Theological Seminary and the men and women of the Adult Bible Class of Central Methodist Church, Skokie, Illinois, in whose company I have learned much about this Gospel.

A sabbatical leave from my teaching duties and spent in Rome has given me the welcome opportunity to prepare this little commentary.

The book was issued originally as a study book for the Women's Society of Christian Service of The United Methodist Church under the title *Coming to Life*. The new edition incorporates a few stylistic alterations and corrections of factual matter. I am grateful for the opportunity presented to address a wider public.

ERNEST W. SAUNDERS

Tis writ, "In the beginning was the Word."
I pause, to wonder what is here inferred.
The Word I cannot set supremely high:
A new translation I will try.
I read, if by the spirit I am taught,
This sense: "In the beginning was the Thought."
This opening I need to weigh again,
Or sense may suffer from a hasty pen.
Does Thought create, and work, and rule the hour?
'Twere best: "In the beginning was the Power."
Yet, while the pen is urged with willing fingers,
A sense of doubt and hesitancy lingers.
The spirit comes to guide me in my need,
I write, "In the beginning was the Deed."

> Johann Wolfgang Goethe, *Faust*.
> trans. Philip Wayne (Harmondsworth,
> Middlesex: Penguin Books, 1951), p. 71.

Chapter ONE

Why Another Gospel?

A NEWCOMER TO THE CHRISTIAN FAITH, or one who stands outside it, might very well put the question, "Why another Gospel? Surely Mark has given a complete enough account of what Jesus of Nazareth, the Galilean teacher, did. If we want a more poetic style and a larger collection of his teachings, we have the records of that doctor-historian—Luke. Since Matthew presents the case from the standpoint of Jewish converts to the Church, why another Gospel? Why four? And why stop there? Why not five?"

Such questions are not as modern as they sound. As the New Testament began to be assembled, early Christians had to face the same embarrassment over plural accounts of the mission of Jesus. Luke heard these questioning criticisms, as the preface to his Gospel makes plain (Luke 1:1-4). Sometimes they took the form of taunts intended to ridicule the strange Syrian cult that had begun to push across the Roman Empire. One outspoken pagan critic of Christianity in the late second century (quoted by a Christian teacher of Alexandria) accused the Christians of treating their gospel "like drunkards . . . recoining it three and four and many times."[1]

Puzzled about the duplicate and divergent narratives in the latter part of the second century one

1

Christian leader, Tatian, even attempted to merge the separate Gospels into a single running account which would present the one gospel more completely. But he never attracted much of a hearing. The four Gospels had already won a secure position in the faith and life of the Church before his time, and there was little question about their place in the developing canon. Irenaeus of Lyons, a bishop in Gaul, expressed the conclusions of others when he pointed out that there was a basic unity among these four different reports, for they represented the one gospel under four aspects.[2]

This is not to deny that each Gospel has its own undeniable individuality. What then is the special contribution of the Fourth Gospel? What did its author have in mind? Did he want to fill in some of the obvious gaps in the story told by the other evangelists? Or was it his intention to produce a fuller description and a more probing analysis of "the things which have been accomplished among us," which would replace the existing reports? We can only speculate about his opinions of the other Gospels, if he had any, but a careful reading of John's work, viewed in the light of the missionary extension of the church in his day, can help us appreciate some of his more important concerns.

A Fresh Approach to the Ministry of Jesus

Our writer makes no secret of what he is about. He states frankly and openly the implicit purpose behind each of the other Gospels. Admitting that his is a highly selective account of a lifework which could be more exhaustively dealt with, he confides why he has chosen what he has to tell.

> These are written that you may believe that Jesus is the Christ [that is to say, the Messiah of Old Testament promise], the Son of God, and that believing you may have life in his name. — *John* 20:31

Straightforward and matter of fact enough. He is neither a dispassionate chronicler nor a reporter aspiring to literary honors. He has a propagandist's zeal, an enthusiast's conviction, and an avowed missionary purpose. He intends to persuade us that he has a message of singular importance which is of the greatest possible urgency and significance for all who listen.

But then, so do the other evangelists. Why another Gospel? Searching for an answer to our question, Clement of Alexandria, another renowned early Christian leader, put it this way:

> But, last of all, John, perceiving that the external facts had been made plain in the gospel, being urged by his friends, and inspired by the Spirit, composed a spiritual gospel.[3]

Probably Clement had in mind a special meaning when he used the word "spiritual," implying thereby that the Fourth Gospel was written in order to counteract the Gnostics heretical interpretation of the life and teachings of Jesus. At many points John will be heard in protest against the advocates of a special heavenly knowledge called gnosis, although he was apparently influenced by some of the views current in Gnostic circles. Basically, however, Clement perceived that this Gospel writer aimed at a penetrating re-examination of some of the scenes of Jesus' ministry from a theological point of view. He wished to discover and to demonstrate how every word and every act reflected the glory of the One who was truly the Son of God.

In John's day and in ours a line of distinction is often drawn between the Palestinian ministry of the Galilean and the activity of the risen Lord in the Church. The teacher-prophet of Nazareth, located as a historical figure in time and place, seems to bear little relationship to the glorified heavenly Lord whose unseen but real presence empowers the believer and inspires the Church throughout the ages. John is convinced that one cannot correctly understand Jesus of Nazareth unless one sees in his every word and act the Christ of Easter. The Christ of the Church's adoration and faith is none other than the Galilean prophet fully understood. The One who is now coming to his own is the One who once came and who will come again at the end. John wished to make it clear who Jesus really was and to show his permanent significance for faith. Therefore, John set his account of the living Lord (known through Christian experience) in the form of a historical narrative of Jesus' days in the flesh.

WHY ANOTHER GOSPEL? 5

In one sense his presentation of the earthly Jesus as the victorious Son of God makes Jesus seem less real and human to us. As one scholar says,

> Jesus strides with confidence through the pages of the Gospel of John to his appointed end, fully master of the whole situation and of every incident, and sublimely independent of everyone else.[4]

The writer, in his concern to demonstrate the glory of God manifest in everything Jesus said and did, omits crucial episodes like the birth, the baptism, the Transfiguration, the institution of the Lord's Supper, and the agony in Gethsemane. Did John feel they were incompatible with his understanding of the Incarnate Word?

It is very important to observe, however, that the Christ of the Fourth Gospel is no angelic visitant, no celestial superman who had no real human existence. He is revealed as a real person precipitating positive and negative reactions in face to face encounters with people. His reactions of deep disturbance over the savagery of illnesses crippling human life, his turmoil of decision as he faces the cross, his grief displayed over the death of Lazarus—these are genuine, not imitation, emotions.

By showing the essential relationship of the living and present Lord to the history of God's acts in Israel, this Gospel deepens our understanding of Christ as the key to the meaning of history. By interpreting and affirming the relationship of the

Christ-of-faith to the Jesus-of-history, it denies and guards against the view that Christ was a divine being who did not really share all the trials and tribulations of ordinary human living. By insisting that this very real person who lived and worked in Judea and Galilee was the authentic disclosure of God present among men, John makes it clear that the Christian life is not to be confused with a vague mystical rapture but is the obedient acceptance of a definite and demanding way of life.

Facts and Faith

Already we are better prepared to understand how this Gospel takes its place with the other three. John's account of Jesus' message and mission is even more interpretative and evaluative. We might compare the form of this Gospel with T. S. Eliot's play, *Murder in the Cathedral*, rather than with the historian's account of the conflict between Henry II and the Archbishop of Canterbury. It differs from the Synoptic Gospels[5] in the way George Bernard Shaw's play, *Saint Joan*, differs from a chronicle of the wars between France and England in the fifteenth century, or in the way an artist's portrait differs from a photographer's candid camera shot. The analogies are only suggestive, of course, for each of the Gospels is an interpretative study in its own way.

It is surprising to discover how much of the material in this Gospel is without any duplication in the others. A check will show that about ninety-three percent of the contents is special to it. Only John, for instance, tells us about the earliest phase of Jesus' work in Judea before John the Baptist was arrested by the police of Herod Antipas. He is the only one of the writers to extend the ministry of Jesus to a period of over two years in length, perhaps even three if the feast in 5:1 refers to Passover. The cleansing of the Temple introduces the public ministry of Jesus in this Gospel; it comes in the closing week in the others.

There are new stories such as the sign performed at the wedding feast at Cana (2:1-12); the healing of a chronic invalid at the pool of Bethesda (5:1-18); and the raising of Lazarus (11:1-44). None of the familiar parables found in the Synoptic Gospels appears here, but John gives us the well-known figures of Christ as the Good Shepherd (10:1-21), and the true Vine (15:1-17). Conversations are recorded with the heretical Jews of Samaria (4:4-42) and with a group of Greeks who approach Jesus at Passover time (12:20-36).

Nevertheless it is apparent that the writer is acquainted with the basic tradition of Jesus' ministry embodied in the Synoptic Gospels. He may have known the Gospel of Mark, and some scholars think he shows some indebtedness to material found in Luke. But the relationships do not admit of precise identification. It may be that he drew upon recollections, traditions, and sources parallel to those used by Mark and Luke. One can conclude that, while John utilized sayings and episodes from the ministry of Jesus similar to those familiar to the other Gospel writers, he also wove into his theological study some entirely new material—factual matters and interpretations of Jesus and his teaching—and recast everything to fit the special pattern and purpose of his work. (The recasting was more concerned with purpose than "style," though it naturally affected both.)

Since the total work possesses the style of a coherent unified literary composition, it is often difficult to know where John's quotations end and his own reflections begin. For example, what begins as a response to Nicodemus' question, "How can a man be born when he is old?" seems to develop into the author's own Spirit-inspired meditation on the mission of Christ as an expression of the love and judgment of God (3:16-21). In other passages the transition or development is not so readily apparent.

Scholars are by no means agreed upon the historical worth of all this new material. There are those who believe that this Gospel enshrines some exact sayings of Jesus otherwise unknown and that the events recorded constitute primary biographical material for any survey of Jesus' career. Though agreeing that he used some early traditional materials, other commentators are convinced that the writer of the Fourth Gospel is more concerned with an understanding and interpretation of Jesus' historical ministry in the light of faith, and the attempt to show that the historical Jesus is the very same Christ who is known in Christian experience. They regard the special traditions John uses to be of dubious historical worth.

What John gives us to read and ponder is certainly something other than a biographical study with slavishly-literal quotations and journalistically-recorded events. Facts and figures, though not ignored, never determine the presentation. In fact the story as such is subordinated to the presentation of a doctrine of Christ as the revealer and to the revelation of the life and truth he brings. John writes a theological history, selecting those scenes and sayings in which by faith the reader can perceive the presence and action of the living God. "That you [YOU] may believe."

To a modern world increasingly reliant upon audio-video tapes, and electronic instruments for making records, John's way of presenting the story of Jesus may seem strange. But he knew that a literal reproduction of Jesus' words and deeds was not what was needed. It was much more important that the faithful disciple should have the mind of Christ, so that his grasp of the meaning of Jesus' life and death could guide him to a free rendering of the teachings for new situations in a different time.

In this sense we can find deep insight in the Alexandrian teacher's words. Clement is right. This is truly a *spiritual* Gospel. Its unrivaled position in the affection of Christian folk through the ages—from the illiterate beginner in the faith to the learned theologian—is verification of that. Small wonder, then, that John has been hailed as perhaps the greatest theologian in all the history of the Church. Luther regarded his Gospel as the unique and truly pre-eminent Gospel.

The Gospel and the Search for Life

The author of this Gospel, like his Lord, was very much concerned about the age-old quest for a life that has purpose and meaning. How do you find such a life? That is the question. Ponce de Leon looked for it in one way. He thought that if you could find an elixir which would arrest the normal aging process then life would be ensured. The Fountain of Youth still beguiles us. The great American dream of comfortably-padded living is essential to vast worlds of advertising, entertainment, cosmetics, and gadgetry of all sorts. The dean of the Harvard Divinity School, Dr. Samuel H. Miller, has analyzed our sensate culture:

> A brand of tobacco makes a wisp of a fellow feel like a dauntless he-man; a kind of whiskey becomes the stamp of explorers and daredevils; a face cream turns an ugly duckling into a princess in one application; a detergent properly used resolves all the drudgery and nasty housewifely duties into a paradise of uninterrupted bliss. Salvation was never more ardently proffered by the church in its most fervent evangelism to save the world than it is now by frenetically hepped-up hucksters, who promise the full delight of heaven to those who are bored in

their chrome-plated hell, by giving them
more of the same sort of thing.[6]

But life and salvation still elude us as the psychotherapists and the barbiturate manufacturers testify. The conclusion of the modern "theater of the absurd" and the existentialist writers is that man deceives himself cruelly by trying to make sense out of all this nonsense of life. He might as well face the fact that life is largely a hoax, crammed with absurdities of every sort from beginning to end. Once a man has the courage to acknowledge that staggering fact, he is prepared to come to terms with it, not necessarily by denying all beliefs and values, but by the "acceptance of the desperate encounter between human inquiry and the silence of the universe."[7] He is alone and on his own. It is a sign of childishness to search the skies for help.

John proposes another way to come to maturity. One who came from the presence of God himself broke into the drabness and aimlessness of human living and disclosed an entirely new possibility. The Fourth Gospel speaks of it as eternal life. The rabbis had talked about it. When the Holy One of Israel ushered in the World to Come, they agreed, blessedness, righteousness, and peace would prevail everywhere on earth. Men would rejoice in this *chayai ha'olam hab'ba,* literally, "the life of the world to come." The earliest of our Gospels already associates this life with the coming kingdom of God (Mark

9:45, 47; 10:30), but it is our Gospel which focuses upon it as the heart and center of Jesus' message to men. "I have come that men may have life, and may have it in all its fullness" (John 10:10, N.E.B.). His task is to make it available to men; he is the representative of God in bringing this life into the world. "I give them eternal life" (10:28).

But this Gospel is not to be another theological discussion about the World to Come debated in a rabbinical college. To John and to the early church, Jesus in himself was the actual demonstration of that new reality. He himself was that life become flesh and blood (11:25; 12:50; 14:6). To share in it is to become involved with him in an attachment of personal loyalty and an obedience to all that he commands. *The revelation does not consist of a doctrine but a relationship.* "This is eternal life: to know thee who alone art truly God, and Jesus Christ whom thou hast sent" (17:3, N.E.B.). There is no true knowing which is not also a following, and no knowing or following which does not open new vistas of possibility for meaningful existence.

In the Vatican Museum of Christian Art, there is a fragment of gilt engraved glass found in the catacombs which speaks of this ancient longing for life. It takes the form of two words: *Vita Tibi*, (Life to you)! That is man's hope and Christ's promise.

The wonder of it all is that this is no longer an idea to be discussed or a hope to be dreamed about, but a reality to be experienced *now*.

> In very truth, anyone who gives heed to what I say and puts his trust in him who sent me has hold of eternal life, and does not come up for judgement, but has already passed from death to life. — *John* 5:24, N.E.B.

Hope has been realized; the future has become present, and John celebrates it as a glad reality. God has done this for men because he is that kind of God, patient, understanding, disciplining, gracious. As the Bible insists everywhere, he is a God concerned that men shall not die but live. The message of the Gospel of John is that when men meet this God and assume responsibility for themselves before him, then they are set free for a new future no longer burdened by their past.

John understood man's instinctive fear of darkness and his insatiable love of light. He believed that the real truth had been found, a truth not expressible in the formal commandments of the Law from Sinai nor capable of formulation in the propositions of philosophic reasoning, but bound instead in the shape of a human life. In Christ there was real life and that life is the true light guiding men through the darkness of this world. The truth men look for is to be found here in the revealing words spoken by this Galilean and in the whole movement of his life, for that life was nothing other than the most high God become present in this ordinary human world.

A Word About His First Readers

Since this ought to be a welcome word of the greatest importance to everyone, John probably imagined no restrictions on the circle of his readers. Members of little congregations of believers like his own were always in need of guidance and counsel. Some of them could recite the plain facts of the ministry of Jesus—they had been attentive students during their probationary period of instruction. But they had only a meager understanding of the inner meaning of that life for the ultimate issues of life and death, heaven and earth, freedom and bondage.

Some of them were not even sure of the importance of Jesus' ministry for their present experience of Christ. With some embarrassment they wondered how the heavenly Son of God could ever have been subject to the limitations of ordinary human life in an obscure province of the eastern Roman Empire. They listened with growing approval to certain Christian teachers, claiming to possess a secret heavenly knowledge or gnosis, who maintained that the heavenly Lord had only *seemed* to possess human characteristics. Actually, this would have compromised his deity. At the other extreme were some Jewish Christians who thought of Christ as the greatest of the prophets—human, not divine, though divinely inspired—and who were clinging to many of their former customs and ceremonies.

John believed both of these views of Christ were

inadequate, and his own interpretation aims to correct the misunderstandings of both Gnostic and Ebionite Christians. A deeper understanding of who Christ is, why he came, and what he did, would go a long way toward solving the problems of division within the congregations, the shallowness of spiritual life among the members, careless and unworthy leadership, and a half-magical view of the sacraments of Baptism and the Holy Supper.

In part, too, John was determined to expose the errors of the critics of the church in his day. The synagogues continued in conflict with the struggling Christian societies. From the Jewish standpoint it was plain nonsense at the least and dire blasphemy at the most to argue that God's salvation could be present in the tragic career of a messianic pretender. The most vigorous repudiation of Judaism anywhere in the New Testament is found in the work of this evangelist. Unfortunately it has sometimes given the impression of an anti-Semitic bias which has offended some readers and pleased others. The "Nordic Christianity," promoted by Alfred Rosenberg in the interests of Hitler's Third Reich, is a horrible example of a perverted faith claiming the support of this Gospel.

Apparently John was also concerned to deny the claims of some enthusiastic followers of John the Baptist who were convinced that their martyred leader was the true prophet Moses had foretold (Deut. 18:15-18) or even the messianic leader himself. In this Gospel the Baptist minimizes his own role in the events leading up to the end of the world and the wrath to come, insisting that he was definitely not the awaited Messiah (John 1:20), nor even the Elijah-prophet of Malachi's prediction (1:21). In his own words he is simply an anonymous voice crying in the wilderness (1:23).

John's Gospel, then, was intended to serve a variety of needs. Apathetic Christians needed to be brought to their senses. New Christians required counsel about the way of discipleship and a growing knowledge of Christ. Heretical views had to be challenged and refuted. The malicious attacks of the enemies of the faith had to be broken. And withal, those who had never heard the good news of God's act in Jesus Christ, both Jews and Romans, must be evangelized. These are not essentially different from the responsibilities that face every Christian who takes seriously his commitment to live in the world and serve Christ today. Evangelism, the strengthening of community life, education, defense and interpretation of doctrine —these are the common and continuing tasks that confront the church. A great deal can be learned from the way this early Christian pastor-missionary-theologian goes about them. Members of Christ's community of faith today are trying to grasp anew the meaning of Christ for their world and to deepen their faith in him as the manifestation of God's love for his creation.

Introducing the Author

Along with the other evangelists, the author of this Gospel must have felt that the message he had to proclaim was of far greater consequence than advertising his own identity. Not one of the writers of the gospel history signed his name to his publication. The story was no personal possession of theirs for which they could take credit. It was the common property of the whole fellowship of believers with whom they stood as brothers in Christ. Years later Christians began to be curious about the writers who had transmitted this common Christian tradition. Irenaeus of Lyons, writing *ca* A.D. 180, assumed that the writer of the story was a disciple and confidant of Jesus; namely, John, the son of a Galilean fisherman named Zebedee. This quickly became the traditional view in Christian circles. It did not go unchallenged, however. A Christian group of that time disparagingly referred to as the Irrationalists (*Alogi*), and a few years later, a certain church official at Rome named Gaius, questioned the orthodoxy of the Gospel. They contended that it was the composition of a notorious Jewish-Christian Gnostic teacher of Alexandria, named Cerinthus.[8] Others, too, doubted that the Apostle's name should be connected with it, though they accepted it as an authoritative account of the mission of Jesus.

The church group responsible for the publication of this Gospel appended a note of endorsement when it was sent out, commending it as the work of one of Jesus' disciples. "This is the disciple who is bearing witness to these things, and who has written these things; and we know that his testimony is true" (21:24). Here we must begin to do some literary detective work since the disciple is not named. It looks as though the so-called beloved disciple is referred to, one of the twelve who is mentioned in this affectionate way several times in the later chapters (13:23; 19:26; 20:2; 21:7, 20). But our problems have only begun, for, despite the long tradition in the Church naming John as the beloved disciple, the Gospel itself never identifies him. Of all the possibilities proposed—and they include candidates like Lazarus, Nicodemus, and the Rich Young Ruler —John, the son of Zebedee is indeed the most likely. If so, the endorsement means that he is believed to be the author of the Gospel.

In modern times some students of this Gospel, unable to associate a sophisticated Greek interpretation of the Palestinian Gospel with a simple Galilean fisherman, have proposed that the real author was an early church official who bore the same given name as the apostle. They think an elder of Ephesus named John was confused with his teacher, John the Apostle. Confusion of mistaken identifications of leaders with the same names sometimes did occur.[9] Others despair of fixing his name. They are content to conclude that he was an unknown friend and pupil of the apostle John from whom he learned much. After the aged apostle's death, his friend composed this study, combining some of the traditions common to the other writers with reminiscences of his own teacher, the whole infused with his own deep insights into the real meaning of what happened in Galilee.

The evidence is not conclusive for any single position and we propose to leave the matter open. But in all probability the writer must take his place with many nameless saints of Christian history whose right to remembrance rests on what they did rather than who they were. If we may suppose that he was a disciple and confidant of the aged apostle John, indebted to him for some of these recollections and explanations, then there is substance in the traditional conviction of an apostolic authority behind this interpretative memoir.[10]

If we cannot be certain about the author's exact name, we can still learn a great deal about him from what he writes and the way he writes. There is no doubt that he is a person well read in that diluted Greek culture known as Hellenism and in Hellenistic Judaism. He has a real interest in the popular Jewish festivals like Passover, Sukkoth, and Hanukkah, and believes that their inner significance has been fulfilled in Christ. His familiarity with the Logos concept, used extensively by the Stoic philosophers and by Philo, a brilliant Jewish philosopher of Alexandria, bears witness to his acquaintance with Hellenistic religious philosophy. And there are hints here and there of a knowledge of the Roman mystery cults as well as the technical theological vocabulary of Gnostic theosophy.

No recluse from society, he was a Christian conversant with the dominant culture of his day who presented the significance of Christ in the highest categories of thought his culture could provide. Perhaps the immediate background of his thought can best be understood in terms of that wider Judaism of the Dispersion exhibited in writings like the *Wisdom of Solomon* in the Apocrypha, the letters of Paul, and the treatises of Philo.

His writing reflects the mental and artistic qualities of a theological poet; it is discerning, intuitive, mystical, dramatic, unitive. He delights in the use of antitheses, drawing sharp contrasts between truth and falsehood, light and darkness, heaven and earth (above and below), life and death, freedom and bondage. As in the morality plays and *Pilgrim's Progress*, the characters in his drama are often personifications of personality types or qualities. Nicodemus is a symbol of the friendly Jewish intellectual; the Samaritan woman represents the Samaritan mission, long since begun by the time John writes; Thomas serves as an example of the many Christians who insist on some visible evidence to prove the validity of their faith.

One of the fascinating features of the author's style is his use of words deliberately chosen for their ambiguous meanings; the extensive use of what the French call *double entendre* or double meanings surely cannot be accidental. In the exchange between Jesus and the notable rabbi Nicodemus, for example, there is a play of meanings upon the Greek adverb *anōthen*. Nicodemus understands it in the sense of "again" and asks with sarcasm how a man can be born a second time. The reply of Jesus shows that he does not intend a temporal meaning at all, but spatial. The word *anōthen* can be used legitimately to mean "from above," and that is the sense conveyed by the context of Jesus' words. Physical birth is something involuntary and universal, but birth from above, birth by the Spirit, must be chosen and not all men are open to it.

We must be on the alert for this kind of semantic subtlety as we go along in our reading of John's Gospel or we shall miss much of his meaning. Many words are chosen to convey meanings on several different levels, words like: to lift up, to raise up, to live, to die, to see, to send, to follow, to fulfill, bread, water, blindness, health and many others. In the story of the high priest Caiaphas addressing the official Jewish council with the observation, "It is expedient for you that one man should die for the people, and that the whole nation should not perish" (11:50), there is more intended by the evangelist than a death warrant safeguarding these leaders from Roman reprisals. John contrives this ambiguous statement to make even this chief enemy an unconscious prophet of Christ's vicarious death for the sin of the world.

This veiled manner of speech may be seen in a number of episodes related to the ministry of Jesus which are to be read as symbolic narratives, based in many cases upon historical material. Through the story of Jesus' curing a case of congenital blindness, the reader is encouraged to recognize that Jesus' presence in the world brings men out of spiritual blindness into a full vision of reality. Implicit in the story of the postponement of the physical death of one man, Lazarus of Bethany, is the message which affects us all. We should realize that Jesus Christ *is* the resurrection and the life, robbing death of its power to terrify and destroy us. If we have eyes to see we shall recognize something far more significant in the Cana miracle than Jesus' enjoyment of village merrymaking at a wedding by replenishing an exhausted wine supply! This writer's skill in communicating with us on more than one level of meaning makes his study endlessly intriguing and inspiring to "all sorts and conditions of men." [11]

A Few Facts and Figures (for the scientifically minded)

Not so long ago it was rather commonly believed that this work originated last of all the Gospels, well into the second century, in the city of Ephesus in western Asia Minor. Several discoveries have prompted a revision of this view.

For one thing, we have manuscript evidence to show that by the early part of the second century this Gospel was already known and in use among Greek-speaking Christians of Egypt. The oldest fragment we possess of any portion of the New Testament is a piece of papyrus, 3½ by 2½ inches in size, found in the Fayyum district of Egypt and dated about

A.D. 130.[12] It contains five verses from the eighteenth chapter of John. Another group of papyrus scraps, which seem to represent a blend of stories from all the Gospels, also can be dated a decade or so before the middle of the second century.[13] If our Gospel was not composed in North Africa, but appeared there at such an early date, it is reasonable to suppose that it was written close to the turn of the century or even in the last years of the first century.

A far more significant find related to the earliest form of this Gospel did not become public knowledge until 1956. Several years before, newspapers reported the sensational news that a wealthy Swiss business man and book collector, M. Martin Bodmer, had acquired a papyrus codex of the Gospel of John which was complete for fourteen chapters and contained substantial parts of remaining chapters. Subsequently a second copy of the same Gospel was identified amid the hoard of papyrus leaves M. Bodmer had purchased in Cairo.[14] Dated about A.D. 200, these two books give us the oldest continuous text of John's work that we have. These are several centuries earlier than our oldest copies of Matthew and Mark. Here again the circulation of this Gospel in Egypt at this time appears to support a date of composition somewhere between A.D. 95 and 120.

Much better known among recent discoveries of ancient manuscripts are the celebrated scrolls from the desert community of Qumran by the Dead Sea. One of the truly surprising results of a study of the sectarian documents of this Jewish monastic center is the remarkable kinship between certain aspects of the theology of Qumran and the teaching represented in the Gospel of John. Particularly noticeable are the parallel ways in which they describe the struggle between light and darkness, truth and falsehood. Even the expressions "spirit of truth" and "holy spirit" appear in the *Manual of Discipline*.

But there are, of course, profound differences. To the monks of Qumran, God's judgment is yet to come and the victory yet to be decided. To John and the Christian community, the world is already judged and the victory has already been decided in the Resurrection. At Qumran one became a son of light by a faithful study of and submission to the precepts of the Law of Moses. For John that new life comes by faith in Jesus Christ who replaces the Torah. "The law was given through Moses; grace and truth came through Jesus Christ" (1:17).

It is argued by some that these theological resemblances suggest an origin for the Gospel of John somewhere in Syria or Palestine. But it is just as possible that Qumran theology was not unknown in Asia Minor, perhaps through the sect of John the Baptist which was represented in Alexandria and Ephesus (Acts 18:24f.; 19:1f.).

But these are all introductory considerations. Why another Gospel? The answer to that question will not be found by turning our study into an Agatha Christie story of mystery and detection, nor by succumbing to what one scholar has called parallelomania, that is, tracing out parallel words and thoughts in other documents. We must let the writer tell us in his own words what he has to say and then reflect upon it, critically and prayerfully. Then we are prepared to understand why he believed the story had not yet been told in all its grandeur and glory. Indeed we shall hear him admit before he is through that a single book could never contain all that Jesus did and signifies. "Jesus did many other signs in the presence of the disciples which are not written in this book" (John 20:30). For, he might tell us, Christ is greater than anything and everything that can be said about him.

> They are but broken lights of thee,
> And thou, O Lord, art more than they.
> — *Alfred, Lord Tennyson*

Chapter TWO

What's The Good Word?

A SKILLED BOOK REVIEWER always pays careful attention to the preface of a book. Long experience has trained him to recognize in these opening pages what to expect from the chapters that follow. As many an author can testify, happily or ruefully, a book can be made or broken by its opening. Here his point of view and the plans he expects to follow are set before the reader, for better or for worse. Often enough it is the last thing he does, and perhaps with most worry and care.

In the case of the Gospel according to St. John, it was a stroke of sheer inspiration that fashioned these first paragraphs (eighteen verses) and set them as the heading for the story to be told. With staccato precision and tonal clarity, they announce at the very beginning the principal themes which will be taken up for varied restatement by this master-composer.

A Hymn in Praise of Christ the Word

A writer can choose a thousand different ways to begin his work. In the case of the Gospel writers, there are several approaches. Mark, the earliest, identifies the beginning of the good news with the prophetic preaching of John the Baptist. As for Matthew and Luke, each tells his own version of the nativity story in a narrative form. John opens his hymn book and copies out the words of an early Christian hymn, meditating upon its cadences and annotating the text as he goes along. From his Jewish background he had learned the faith of Israel set to music. The matchless collection of poetry and hymnody represented in the Psalter was but a single example of the many spiritual songs in which he, and his fathers before him, had lifted up their praise and adoration to the Fount of Blessing.[1]

The early church was a singing church, too. The Roman governor of Bithynia-Pontus in Asia Minor at the beginning of the second century described the worship practices of the Christians in his district in a letter written to the Emperor Trajan (A.D. 98-117):

> They were in the habit of meeting on a certain fixed day before it was light, when they sang in alternate verses a hymn to Christ, as to a god. . . .[2]

The summary statements in I Corinthians 14:26, Colossians 3:16, and Ephesians 5:19 about Christian "psalms, hymns, and spiritual songs" may be illustrated in the nativity hymns such as Mary's song (Luke 1:46-55) inserted into Luke's account of the birth of Christ, the hymn on the Incarnation in Philippians 2:6-11, and the majestic choruses of The Revelation (e.g. Rev. 5:9-10) which found incomparable musical settings in Handel's well-known oratorio.

So John commences his own account of the saving act of God in Jesus Christ, not with a description of the desert prophet of righteousness, nor with a story about the circumstances of the birth of a baby, but with a *song of praise*. For so, in the opinion of many scholars, we are to understand the literary form of the opening eighteen verses of chapter one. The Greek text, echoing the rhythmic patterns of Hebrew poetry, consists of eleven couplets which can be divided into three strophes. As we shall see, the rhythm is interrupted in several places where the evangelist inserts his own comments upon the words.[3]

It may well be that the hymn is an adaptation (by the writer or his source) of a still earlier Greek-Jewish hymn in praise of the Heavenly Wisdom or the holy Torah. Whatever the origin, what matters most is *the meaning John finds* in the traditional phrases and how he uses them to give expression to his own faith in Christ as the sign of God's presence in a new way in the world. It is as though one were to introduce a study of the life of Christ with a stanza or two from "All Hail the Power of Jesus' Name!" With that jubilant apostrophe of praise, one is ready to begin a task which is less adaptable to the limitations of narrative prose than to the poetic images of a doxology!

The Gospel in a New Key

Before we look more carefully at each of the verses in the prologue-hymn we must give attention to the dominant theme which is the center of the whole piece. What is in a word? Nothing—if we do not grasp what lies behind it. Everything—if we reach through it to locate the reality it points to. The language of a letter or a poem may be deceptively simple until we pause to reflect on how it is used, on the changes in the meaning of common words which have been introduced over centuries of communication, and on the special significance the writer may intend. Take the case of the Greek word *logos* which is usually translated into English as "word." A rich and storied history lies behind this simple expression that John takes up as a concept for interpreting Christ.

The early Christian Church summarized in this term *logos* its conviction that the total event of Jesus Christ was a revelation of the God who fulfills his promise to visit and redeem his people. The Word of God for these believers was never frozen into the pages of a book, piously displayed but seldom opened or comprehended. They thought of the Word of God as that living, moving, judging, redeeming action of God which actually took place in the human life of Jesus of Nazareth. With keen insight into the biblical meaning of the word, the German poet Goethe translated *logos* with the German word *Tat*, a "deed" or "act."[4] That is exactly what John meant. Jesus Christ was the human *act* of God. Paul was saying this when he spoke of the "word of the cross," the "word of the truth" and the "word of reconciliation" (see I Cor. 1:18; II Cor. 5:19 K.J.V.; Col. 1:5).

The Word was God's language addressing men. He did not speak in some foreign and incomprehensible tongue, nor with the expertise of the intellectual aristocrat or priestly favorite. No, God spoke in the simple speech of common humanity so that all men could hear and grasp what he had to say. Jesus Christ is that word of truth, John believes, and those who recognize him for who he is can hear it. (John 5:24, 37f.; 8:31f., 43).

But the term *logos* was not freshly minted by either the early church or John. It had long been a part of the religious vocabulary of Hellenism and Judaism. It was the coin of Olympus and Sinai as well as Calvary. A part of the lexicon of philosophy in circulation since the days of the philosophers Heraclitus and Plato, it had come into new circulation in the empire through Stoic teaching. Set in a bewildering complexity of meanings, *logos* signified essentially for the Stoic the divine Reason at the center of the universe. Like Fire, Providence, and Destiny, it was one of the ways of referring to the ultimate ground of all things, the Intelligence and Power that sustained the rational system of visible things. As rational creatures men shared it. As seminal Reason, the *logos* imparted order upon nature and inspired men to seek after the highest moral and intellectual values. The wandering Stoic evangelists who travelled from city to city in the empire preached the virtue of a life which was in harmonious adjustment to this rational principle.

The Jewish conception of *logos* (*dabar*, in Hebrew) was decidedly different. The emphasis here was not upon a contemplation of the divine principle of reason and a proper interpretation of reality, but upon coming to know the divine will and giving it appropriate expression in conduct. It was *the world of energy and action* rather than *thought and contemplation* which engaged the concern of Israel. When the Jew spoke of the Word of God he had in mind the wondrous creative power of God that brought the world out of the darkness of primordial chaos into order and light. He celebrated in songs of praise the God who did such wonderful things:

> Rejoice in the Lord, O you righteous!
> Praise befits the upright.
> . . . .
> By the word of the Lord the heavens were
>   made and all their host by the breath of
>   his mouth [*i.e.* his Spirit].
> . . . .
> Let all the earth fear the Lord,
>   let all the inhabitants of the world stand
>   in awe of him!
> For he spoke, and it came to be;
>   he commanded, and it stood forth.
> — *Psalm* 33:1, 6, 8-9[5]

But the God of Israel and the nations was not a kind of cosmic clockmaker who had set the universe running and now busied himself with other more important matters. He continued to speak to men through the mouths of those whom he summoned and sent as his emissaries. "Now the word of the Lord came to me saying . . ." is the authoritative claim Jeremiah makes as he prophesies to Israel (Jer. 1:4; cf. Isa. 55:11; Ezek. 1:3). The *dabar Yahweh* [word of God] is the sign of God's revelational activity as he breaks the silence of the heavens and addresses men in words of judgment and mercy. An eminent modern Jewish theologian, the late Martin Buber, has phrased it well: "Revelation is summons and sending."

In the contact with other cultures, Jewish theology of the postexilic period had further refined its understanding of the divine activity in creation and revelation, personifying this energetic action in the figure of Wisdom, called in Hebrew *hokhmah* and in Greek *sophia*.

> When he established the heavens, I [i.e. Wisdom] was there,
> when he drew a circle on the face of the deep,
> when he made firm the skies above,
>
> . . . .
>
> then I was beside him, like a master workman;
> and I was daily his delight,
> rejoicing before him always,
> rejoicing in his inhabited world
> and delighting in the sons of men.
> — *Proverbs* 8:27, 30-31[6]

Now John speaks of this *sophia* in the form of *logos*. Other New Testament writers abstain from the use of the *logos* concept but find *sophia* fulfilled in Christ. Paul, for instance, speaks of Christ as the Wisdom of God.[7]

In Greek Judaism of the Hellenistic and Roman periods, an effort was made to draw upon the resources of pagan religious thought to elucidate the Jewish understanding and experience of God. The best example is found in the voluminous writings of a Jewish philosopher of Alexandria named Philo, a contemporary of Jesus and John. The term *logos* appears over a thousand times in the treatises of Philo (*ca.* 20 B.C.–*ca.* A.D. 50), often in confusing if not contradictory ways. It is significant to our inquiry that *logos* often refers to a subordinate divine being or principle who is the Image of God and who is the Medium or Agent of God in creation or revelation. But Philo would have been shocked by John's bold claim that this heavenly *logos* could take the form of personal, historical existence and become the means whereby God confronted and redeemed a sinful humanity.

Even the rabbis were not unaffected by the *sophia-logos* concept. The bridge had been thrown between the separate worlds of Hellenism and Judaism. As they meditated upon the marvels of the sacred Law or Torah, the theologians of Judaism began to employ the image of Wisdom and Word, *sophia* and *logos*, as a means of speaking of the eternally existent and enduring commandments of the Lord God.

Torah, they taught, was the Wisdom of God. Torah was the very Word of God.[8] Torah gave life to men in this world and in the world to come. Torah was truth and light, the bread and water of life. Thus, they eulogized God's great gift to Israel in the law of Moses.

No, John was not alone in making use of the *logos* concept. But he and the community of faith in which he served used this familiar theological term to proclaim the glory and praise of Christ, the Word of God become blood and bone.[9] To the Greeks he declares: All that you mean by the divine Reason and principle of intelligibility in the world—all this has become manifest in Jesus Christ. Believe and live. To the Jews John testifies: What the psalmists and prophets heard and repeated in the name of Yahweh has now been sent forth in the words and life of a Galilean teacher. To the arguments of rabbinical authorities and the synagogue councils John responds: God spoke to Moses in a law of ordinances. Now he has spoken to us in Jesus Christ, and Christ, not Torah, is the light of the world, the bread of life, the living water. The word once became a book which was a lamp to our feet and a light to our path. Now the Word has become flesh in a man who is the light of the whole world!

Strophe 1. The Word and God
(John 1:1-5 N.E.B.[10])

When all things began, the Word already
   was.
The Word dwelt with God,
and what God was, the Word was.
The Word, then, was with God at the
   beginning,
and through him all things came to be;
no single thing was created without him.
All that came to be was alive with his life,
and that life was the light of men.
The light shines on in the dark,
and the darkness has never quenched it.

Wisdom was said to be present beside God at the moment of creation. The sacred Torah, according to some rabbis, preceded creation. The Word of God, says John, was with God before anything we know had come into being (vs. 1). That Word in some sense is subordinate to the Creator of all things visible and invisible; he was "with God." Nevertheless, though there is a distinction there is no independent existence, as though there were two wholly separate divine beings, God and the Word in coexistence. That would be a denial of monotheism, the belief that reality has its source in one unitary being. "Thus, from the outset we are to understand that the Word has its whole being within Deity," wrote the renowned Archbishop of Canterbury, William Temple, "but that it does not exhaust the being of Deity."[11]

Similar affirmations are made about Wisdom and the Name of God by Jewish thinkers in the period between the Testaments. The difference is that their statements deal largely with abstract attributes to be debated and discussed, while the Word become flesh is a historical reality, a being who invites men into a personal, interactive relationship. And that makes all the difference.

John intuitively recognized the significance of asserting the full deity of the Word. If Christ is a kind of demigod, like the glorified Greek heroes, then it is not the Most High God who speaks in him and our salvation is put in jeopardy. The New Testament faith is squarely stated: no good angel, nor deified martyr, nor inspired teacher has brought the good news of salvation. Paul has it: "All this is from God . . . God was in Christ reconciling the world to himself" (II Cor. 5:18, 19). In John's language it becomes: "He who has seen me has seen the Father" (14:9b).

That divine Word, therefore, could never be regarded as a spectator or an attendant observing whatever God has done or is doing. To be essentially of the same nature and in full relationship with God must be to share his purposes and participate in his work (vss. 2-3). Nothing less. The God of the Bible is no "do-nothing" deity of whom it can only be said, "He is." In point of fact, "He does" would more accurately describe him. So the Word has been creatively involved in every act of God. Wherever God has revealed himself, whether in creation or redemption, his action may be spoken of as an event of the Word which is Christ. Christ was involved in the first creation. Now in this latest Word-event, a new creation is taking place, a second Genesis which brings the first Genesis to completion.

This belief in Christ as the creative Word rules out the idea that the world is the result of spontaneous creation, an accidental arrangement of self-existent atoms out of which the first rudimentary organisms developed. It denies that men create life by their own engineering. They are given it; they receive it (vs. 4). The new creation is God acting in Jesus Christ to awaken men out of false existence into true existence, bringing them out of nothingness into life. For John, the distinctive task of the Word is to make life possible. The Word is the source, the transmitter, and the sustainer of life. The world in which men dwell, and humanity—the inhabitants of that world—have no life in and of themselves apart from him.[12]

Still, that is John's kind of material and human world. What about ours? As our world has become increasingly subject to man's control through his fantastic scientific achievements, God is often pushed farther and farther away from the center of human operations. Many Christians, in fact, draw a neat distinction between the realms of nature and grace, assigning the world of physical matter, atomic research, and applied science to the work of men, while acknowledging God's activity in the realm of human redemption. They think that what men do technologically is their own business. Problems of exploding population, world hunger, wars, armed satellites, diminishing natural resources, are man's own problems to be dealt with as he sees fit. God's legitimate activity, they hold, is limited to a kind of welfare program for individual souls. Little do those who think this way know that they are sponsoring a revised program of an early heresy in the Christian community according to which there were separate sources of creation and redemption! [13]

John anticipates that kind of thinking and repudiates it entirely. "*All* that came to be was alive with his life" (vs. 4, N.E.B.). The God operative in the marvelous intricacy of the physical universe is the very same God who is at work in history. Everyone and everything comes under the claim of the Logos as the Agent of creation and redemption. Men are responsible to him as the Giver of life both for the soil on which they live and for their souls by which they are distinguished as rational, spiritual creatures. In his own way, John is saying something about man's responsibility to be worthy of the authority which God has delegated to him. The original and ultimate proprietor has entrusted man with the governance of his earth.

In dramatic terms John pictures the struggle of human life in this world as a contest between light and darkness (vs. 5). Our uncertainty before pressing decisions, our perplexity about the effect of our actions upon other people, our ignorance about what the future holds, let alone about what our past experience really means—all this indicates that we are men stumbling and groping along all the way.

But God has not forsaken men in their darkness. The Bible celebrates the goodness of God who provides a light for man's way through the darkness. "Thy word is a lamp to my feet and a light to my path," sang the Psalmist (Ps. 119:105).[14] This light to men provided in the Torah was a sign foretelling the wondrous illumination which would mark the New Age or the Kingdom of God. So a later prophet heralded that day when

> The sun shall be no more your light by day,
> nor for brightness shall the moon give light
>   to you by night;
> but the Lord will be your everlasting light,
>   and your God will be your glory.
> — *Isaiah* 60:19

We never really come into our own as persons, we can never see clearly, until we see and understand ourselves. That light, that understanding which enables men to see things as they truly are and saves them from stumbling and falling, that light which makes possible the discovery of real life—that is the light come in Christ, says John.[15] Rejoice! Be glad! It is the light bathing the new creation which already scatters the darkness of this present world, a world which can neither comprehend it nor control it.[16]

Having made this affirmation, John pauses to show his reader how all this has been verified in the events which have so recently transpired (vss. 6-8). Some have been daring to compare the work of John the

Baptist with that of Christ, as though John were the greater. But this is a major confusion of their roles, the evangelist believes. John the Baptist was surely a man summoned and sent by God, but he was a herald and a witness to someone greater who followed him.

Strophe 2. The Word and the World (John 1:9-13, N.E.B.)

The real light which enlightens every man
was even then coming into the world.
He was in the world;
but the world, though it owed its being to him,
did not recognize him.
He entered his own realm,
and his own would not receive him.
But to all who did receive him,
to those who have yielded him their
   allegiance,
he gave the right to become children of God,
not born of any human stock, or by the fleshly
   desire of a human father, but the offspring
   of God himself.

In this second stanza our Logos hymn begins to focus on all that the Incarnation means. We have heard that every human being in this world, indeed everything that has any being at all, owes its existence to the creative work of the Logos. All enlightenment originates with him and is available to men (vs. 9). Not that they all acknowledge it. John knows full well the tragic fact of human obstinacy which deliberately shuts itself off from light. Some men prefer to remain in the darkness rather than have their motives and conduct brought under the searching inspection of God's light. But it is at least possible for every man to *understand* who he is, where he comes from, and what he ought to do in this world. It was never intended that he be cruelly abandoned to the darkness of ignorance and deception. If he is not enlightened, it is because he cannot or will not be brought to face the truth about himself.

And now that supernal light, which has always been in the world since its beginning, has come in a new and intense way. Christ's coming means just that. "The real light which enlightens every man was even then coming into the world" (1:9, N.E.B.).[17] And the reaction has been divided (vss. 10-11). This is exactly what happened in the mission of Jesus. There was neither then, nor is there now, anything in his activity or message to command instant and unanimous assent. Even among those who were immediate observers of his healing ministry, and hearers of his challenging parables about the approaching kingdom of God, there was a divided response. In that day some believed and surrendered; others disbelieved and attacked. So it is today. "This is the judgment," John observes later, "that the light has come into the world, and men loved darkness rather than light, because their deeds were evil" (3:19). To say that his own people would not receive him brings to mind Jesus' rejection by his Nazareth friends and neighbors (Mark 6:1-6; cf. Matt. 13:53-58), and the parable of the Wicked Husbandmen (Mark 12:1-12). But John's statement has a broader significance. Since all creation is God's in Christ, it is the entire world of men and human affairs organized in rebellion against him that is envisaged here. "His own world would not [and does not] receive him."

Here we confront the whole mystery of the human will and the nature of decision-making. However we explain it, we do make our own choices and we have to accept responsibility for them. Of course we are affected by the decisions of others and our range of freedom is cramped by them. But the basic human decisions—about a controlling purpose in life, about our beliefs and values, and our disposition towards others—these are within our power to make.

For a moment the hymn to Christ the Word acknowledges sadly the tragic fact of perverted human freedom. Then the hymn rises to a thankful note. If there is a disbelieving, hateful, resistant world, it is still the object of the merciful love of God who wants to draw it back into relationship with him (3:16). And there are those who do respond favorably. They welcome the coming of the light, grateful for release from the stronghold of darkness, willing to face the truth about themselves and to look at themselves by that light. These, says John, are acknowledged as the true children of God (vs. 12).

"Children of God" and hence brethren one of another! Today we sometimes become very sentimental about this matter of universal brotherhood. With one great inclusive sweep of the hand, we gather in all humanity as our brothers and sisters, fellow children of the one Father in Heaven. But it is easier to wave the hand toward other men than to open the hand to them. John and the hymn are more down to earth. Obviously we are all creatures of one Lord and Maker.

But sonship according to the Bible is a gift to be appropriated, not a natural endowment to be taken for granted. We may, or we may not, become children of God. That relationship may be the expression of something *potential* in everyone, to be sure, but it is a relationship of *grace* rather than of *nature*. To the Old Testament writers, Israel's sonship to God signified God's choice and call to service which was to be met with an answering response of filial love and obedience.[18] It is in this sense that John understands sonship.

We may recognize in verse 13 a further personal reflection by the evangelist, distinguishing between these two events of entrance into life for the Christian. There is a natural birth; every human being experiences that. But there is a heavenly birth, too, whereby men *discover their origin, find their purpose,* and *learn the possibilities of their existence.* How one becomes a child of God will be a continuing, developing theme of this Gospel of Eternal Life, as we shall see.

Strophe 3. The Word of God Incarnate
(John 1:14, 16-18, N.E.B.)

So the Word became flesh;
he came to dwell among us,
and we saw his glory,
such glory as befits the Father's only Son,
full of grace and truth.

. . . .

Out of his full store we have all received
  grace upon grace;
*For while the Law was given through Moses,
grace and truth came through Jesus Christ.
No one has ever seen God; but God's only
Son, he who is nearest to the Father's heart,
he has made him known.*

With this stanza, the thought of the hymn rises to its climax. In these simple and profound words all the mystery of Christian faith is concentrated. Paul was content to say that Christ came "in the likeness of sinful flesh" (Rom. 8:3). Guarding against any possibility of minimizing the full humanity of the divine Word, John's confession was that Jesus came into the scene of human affairs as—man (vs. 14a). God revealed himself pre-eminently, not in a statute book, not in a creed or concept, nor in an institution, but in the life of a *man*. It was no ordinary life, but one which exhibited the maturity of a manhood fit for the kingdom of God, "full of grace and truth." "We saw his glory . . . ," we know it, we have received it— that is the voice of actual experience, the confession of all who belong to Christ's community (vs. 14b, N.E.B.).

Now in Christ's appearance God had fulfilled his promise to be present among men. Wisdom was said by Jewish teachers to have tabernacled with Israel, recalling the visible presence of God in the form of the bright cloud over and the fire within the ancient Tabernacle in the wilderness.[19] But great as was the sight of that devouring fire above Mt. Sinai, it paled before the glory of God in the coming of his Son (vs. 14b). "Only Son" is to be understood in the sense of unique, or favorite. It is a term of endearment, parallel to the word "beloved" in the other Gospels (Mark 1:11; 9:7; 12:6 and parallels).

We remember how the Transfiguration experience in the Synoptic Gospels was understood to give witness to the three disciples of the heavenly glory suffusing the figure of the praying Jesus (Mark 9:2-8 and parallels).

In John's Gospel it is the entire life of Jesus, not any single moment, which is an embodiment of the glory of God. In a special way, the climax of his ministry in the crucifixion and exaltation is demonstrative of the divine glory upon him (7:39, 12:16, 23, 27-28; 13:31, 32). He is the new and greater Moses who leads the people of God in the new exodus and establishes the full and final meeting between heaven and earth. Furthermore, he imparts the glory given him to his followers so that they may be brought into that unity which marks the relationship of the Son with the Father (vss. 16-17; cf. 17:10, 22). So man, fallen from his true estate by sin, is crowned again with glory and honor.[20]

In the Old Testament God is said to be "merciful and gracious." (Exodus 34.6 and Psalms 85:10 are examples.) Since the Word is of divine nature, he too is said to be "full of grace and truth" (vs. 14b). Only once again, and in this Prologue, does the word "grace" appear (vs. 17). But the meaning remains as a pervading theme of the Fourth Gospel. The sending of the Son into the world is the expression *par excellence* of the undeserved goodness of God and his love for the world.

The other word, "truth," recurs some twenty-five times in this Gospel. "Truth," for our author is one of the key words that represent the complete Christian revelation. If we restrict its meaning to a philosophical definition, we shall limit and underestimate it sadly. We may argue that a thing is true if it corresponds to reality and is subject to verification, but John is thinking about something far beyond that. Just as *emeth* in the Old Testament, truth in this Gospel signifies primarily the faithfulness of God in keeping his promises and saving his people. In the sense in which it was used in Greek religious philosophy, it meant reality as distinguished from illusion. For John this is the truth spoken by Christ and embodied in him. He not only utters the truth; he *is* the truth (14:6). Those who learn to be and to do the truth are girded by God's trustworthiness and saved from the error and illusion of a false understanding about themselves and their purposes.

What is truth, then? "Thy word is truth" (17:17). It is the whole gospel of salvation revealed by and in Christ and made known to men (14:6; 18:37), not in some grudging, niggardly way but as one gift after another in an incredible generosity (1:16).

The hymn concludes (or perhaps it is John's final comment on the hymn) with a contrast between the work of Moses in the written word and Christ as the living Word. Through the centuries the Law had signified the wisdom and the word of God addressing men and summoning them to loyal obedience. But now the old has given way to the new. In Christ, who is the Word sent forth in flesh and blood, the invisible God has become visible, the remote God has drawn near, the hidden God has emerged out of his hiddenness and has made himself known to men. It is in Christ's life of sacrificial service that we see what grace and truth are all about. Only God can reveal God. That is why the oldest and most correct Greek form of verse 18 differs from nearly all the English translations in saying that the "only God" (not the "only Son") has authoritatively disclosed God.[21] Who else could do it? Christ the Word has become the official interpreter of Almighty God,[22] but in truth it is God himself who speaks in him.

On that lofty note, the hymn is concluded. The song has been sung. What follows will set out, in concrete instances from the ministry of Jesus, all that is gathered up in this confessional statement.

An Afterword

Perhaps the real reason John's representation of Christ as God's Word seems so strange to us and so difficult to understand is just that we and our whole age have almost lost the ability to speak meaningfully and honestly to one another. Dialogue often degenerates into idle chatter. *The real tragedy of modern life, it has been observed, is that man has perfected the means of communication in the most skilled way at just the moment when he really has nothing important to say!*

So much of our speech is dead because we ourselves are dead or in hiding. "Empty phrases" was Jesus' comment about some of the elaborate pietistic language in the lengthy prayers of his day (Matt. 6:7). Whether in church, luncheon clubs, or political assemblies, a gush of words may be offered as a substitute for speech with integrity to back it up. We parrot the phrases of others, making sure first that they are harmless. We make all the acceptable noises with our vocal cords, but *we are not really present in what we are saying.* Our question, *What is in a word?* perhaps ought to be rephrased, *Who is in a word?*

Nowhere does the confusion and emptiness of language become more glaring than in our "god-talk." The problem has engaged the minds of some of our best philosophers of religion and theologians today who are trying to help us understand the meaning and purpose of religious language *so that we may learn to speak honestly and clearly about our beliefs.*[23] There is an urgent need today to develop a Christian speech that will be intelligible and convincing to our non-Christian world, just as John's was for his.[24] Jesus' own words have a disturbing relevance to our condition,

> I tell you, on the day of judgment men will render account for every careless word they utter; for *by your words* you will be justified, and *by your words* you will be condemned.
> — *Matthew* 12:36-37

Language, the power of communication so readily taken for granted, holds the secret of what it means to be a person. In the language-event, as a modern German scholar puts it, individual, separated beings are gathered together into a unity. Something new is created; a collection of individuals becomes a community. Language destroys our isolation and draws us together. It transcends the mystery of our hiddenness from one another revealing who we are and who they are. In that kind of meeting between persons who are willing to stop pretending to be what they are not and who are willing to be truly open to each other, each is changed. When confrontation is honest between black men and white men in modern America, the results are often disturbing, but they hold the only valid promise of a new kind of relationship between the races. On another level many Christians have discovered the community-building power of dialogue in small groups meeting regularly for prayer and discussion.

This amazing capacity of human beings to enter into relationships of understanding among themselves furnishes the clue to John's description of Jesus Christ as God's Word spoken to men. In this act of his Incarnation in Jesus, God breaks the abysmal silence of the universe; he is no longer remote, hidden, inscrutable, inaccessible. He does not speak in some unintelligible way to torment and frighten men. He speaks simply and directly in "the language of essential humanity."[25] Jesus is God's language to men, making plain to those who are willing to hear what God's will and purposes are and how men can be awakened to a creative life in relationship with him.

"What God was, the Word was . . .
So the Word became flesh."

Chapter THREE

The Word in the World

EVERY ONE OF THE GOSPELS associates the beginning of Jesus' ministry with the work of John the Baptist, the desert prophet of the Last Judgment who emerged upon the public scene about A.D. 28 (Luke 3:1). The form of the story as it appears in the Fourth Gospel is striking at two points: (1) the definite subordination of John the Baptist to Jesus, and (2) the notation that for a time the two men carried on concurrent programs.

Jesus and John the Baptist (1:19-34)

From the very first the self-depreciation of the Baptist is evident. Before a group of priests and assistants who are said to have been sent by the Pharisees,[1] John disclaimed with a crescendo of emphasis that he was the Messiah, or the Elijah-prophet predicted by Malachi (Mal. 3:1; 4:5, 6), or even the coming prophet of whom Moses spoke.[2] There would have been no need for John the Baptist to dissociate himself from these figures heralding the beginning of the Judgment and the kingdom of God had there not been some such speculation about him. Luke reports the popular murmurings about John as a possible messianic leader (Luke 3:15; Acts 13:25),

53

and we learn from early Christian documents that there was a group of such believers among the Baptist's followers.[3] John will not even permit himself to be considered as the Prophet of the End, though the Synoptic Gospels represent this role as Jesus' own estimate of John's work.[4] From John's standpoint he is best understood as an anonymous voice crying in the wilderness, warning men of the imminence of the end and calling for a national preparation to meet the Lord who is coming (Isa. 40:3).

A rabbinic saying helps us to appreciate the full force of John's own self-estimate. Observed the third century Rabbi Joshua ben Levi, "Every service which a slave will perform for his master, a disciple will do for his Rabbi, except loosing his sandal thongs." Yet it is precisely that menial task that John feels unworthy to perform for the Coming One who is the Messiah (vs. 27).

The scene of John's preaching and baptizing is laid in the obscure little village of Bethany across the Jordan, perhaps not far from a fording place in the stream northeast of Jericho. The baptism of Jesus by John is assumed but not described. In the Fourth Gospel it is the Baptist himself who makes the identification of Jesus which Mark understands as the Voice from Heaven addressing Jesus (Mark 1:11). Confessing his own faith, that Christ is the new and perfect sacrifice, the author records John the Baptist's announcement, "Behold, the Lamb of God, who takes away the sin of the world!" (vs. 29; cf. 36) In the light of the portrait of John the Baptist in the other

Gospels, it may seem strange to represent him historically as a confessing Christian. Our writer is reading history from a theological perspective. From the standpoint of Easter faith he is convinced that all God's dealings with Israel through Moses and the prophets, rising to a climax in John the Baptist, bear testimony that the supreme event has happened in Jesus Christ. No doubt the symbol of the lamb is an allusion to both the Paschal Lamb (Exod. 12, etc.) and the Suffering Servant of God described in Isaiah 53:7, 12,[5] who was to become the vicarious sacrifice bringing redemption to his people.

At Colmar on the eastern border of France, a famous altar piece painted by the artist Matthias Grünewald in the sixteenth century, depicts John's identification of Jesus as "the Lamb of God." As the Baptist points a long bony finger toward the figure of Jesus, he symbolizes the task of every follower of Jesus to bear witness to the One who is the true Savior of men. "There is the One who delivers us from sin." Jesus is the Spirit-endowed one who is the Messiah and who will bestow upon his followers the inestimable gift of the Holy Spirit (vs. 33). Here is dramatized the whole meaning of evangelism: the direction of others to a meeting with Christ.

The Call of the First Disciples (1:35-51)

We are now told of the call of the first followers of Jesus while he was in the southern part of Palestine. Two of the men are former disciples of John the

Baptist: Andrew and probably John the son of Zebedee (vss. 35-37). In turn they bring along Simon Peter (vs. 42) who is promptly given the nickname "Rock." Shortly afterwards, another Galilean joins the group: Philip of Bethsaida.[6] A friend of Philip's, a certain Nathanael ("God gives"), unmentioned in the Synoptic lists, throws in his lot with the others. At the outset he makes the full confession of faith which the Synoptics put at a later point in the mission and assign to Peter, chief spokesman of the little band. "Rabbi, you are the Son of God! You are the King of Israel!" (vs. 49)

In reply Jesus explains what the Gospel writer believes to be the deeper significance of the title, Son of man, so frequently used in the other Gospels to refer to the glorious heavenly figure who will come at the end of time. Like the ladder of Jacob's vision (Gen. 28:12), Jesus is the one who really is the point of contact between high heaven and this earth. He is the eternal intermediary making possible here and now the meeting between God and man and establishing communion between them. Each of the early disciples was convinced of this: "We have found the Messiah!" Therefore, discipleship, following or coming after Jesus, means just this: to recognize in him the truly kingly one who brings righteousness and peace and true life. These are narrative details to be sure, but John uses a narrative approach to write theology. He sees outward events in terms of their inner significance for a truer understanding of the nature and the work of Jesus Christ.

Understanding the Signs of the Time

The word "sign" is very important in John's vocabulary. It is used in several senses, each of which we must examine in the light of the passage in which it is found if we are to understand him. Like the Hebrew *'oth*, the Greek word *sēmeion* is used by John for a symbolic action which points to the purpose of God and gives expression to the divine glory. Recognition of this inner symbolic meaning of Christ's actions can be attained only by perceiving with the "eyes of faith" the invisible spiritual meaning in some observable external event seen with the "eyes of the flesh." If one sees a sign and comprehends its significance and meaning only on the sensory level, he has not yet come to mature faith.

There were many who saw the signs Jesus did at the first Passover feast in Jerusalem. But even though they are said to believe in his name, we learn with surprise that Jesus did not trust himself to them (2:24). Why? Apparently they, like the Pharisees who were forever challenging Jesus to show them a sign from heaven (2:18; Mark 8:11 and parallels),[7] were looking for some kind of physical marvel that would both establish and verify their faith. So Jesus chides the crowd who came looking for him after the lakeside meal because they had not really understood the sign he intended. They only looked for a convenient cheap food supply! (John 6:26)

It is still true today as it was then that many people ask of the Gospels and of Christian faith some observable evidence that will remove all doubt and certify the truth of faith. Faith, to be sure, ought to be open to rational inquiry. "Blind belief" as well as "blind unbelief" is sure to err. But faith is robbed of its true character as faith if it is made subject to external demonstration.

Instead, the Gospel of John describes the signs or works of Jesus which—by the guidance of the Spirit —lead the observer to a true recognition of Jesus as the Revealer of God. The reaction on the part of those who were witnesses to what he did and said ran from one extreme to the other. Some who saw him at work concluded that he was an agent of the Evil One. The sign they saw was Beelzebub in action. Others believed him to be a messianic pretender, or a new prophet, or a wonder-worker, or even the promised royal leader. But the Gospels all agree that *none of these* really saw the true sign.

There were others who became convinced that God's glory was displayed in what Jesus was doing. They perceived in the visible ministry of Jesus of Nazareth the presence of God and his salvation realized among men. This, the Gospels agree in concert, is to recognize the true sign from heaven.

The Sign at Cana: The New Revelation (2:1-12)

Of the many signs which were a part of Jesus' ministry, John singles out seven as representative of the whole. The first of these occurs at a village wedding festival in the Galilean village of Cana before the opening of Jesus' public ministry. Several puzzling aspects of the story have often plagued sincere Christian minds. Why would the Son of God use supernatural power to replenish the refreshments at a village festival? How are we to explain Jesus' brusque if not discourteous reply to his mother's request? Were not similar stories about the conversion of water into wine told of the Greek god Dionysus and celebrated annually at Corinth and Andros?

But we have seen already the way John subordinates incidents and episodes to symbolic and theological interests. A careful rereading will uncover clues which reveal why John tells the story and how he concludes that this was the first sign Jesus performed, manifesting his glory and encouraging in his disciples a deepening of faith (vs. 11). Consider two details: (1) his response to his mother, "O woman, what have you to do with me? My hour has not yet come," (2) the writer's observation that the six huge jars, each holding about twenty or thirty gallons, were for Jewish ceremonial purification purposes.

Some impatience may be evident in Jesus' words, but he is not discourteous.[8] John interprets every incident in Jesus' unfolding ministry with the eventual outcome in view. Accordingly, Mary is reproached for not understanding that the full manifestation of the heavenly glory in her son cannot come before the truly climactic moment. That, as

John sees it, centers in Jesus' death and resurrection. Until that time arrives, the "hour has not yet come" (2:4, repeated again in 7:30 and 8:20). From the standpoint of the unbelieving world, the cross is the evidence of tragedy and political retribution. Seen in the divine plan of redemption, it is a disclosure of the full glory of God.

In the jars of water changed into an enormous amount of wine, the evangelist probably saw the transformation of the old revelation at Sinai into the new revelation at Golgotha. Nor is this so strange. In the Synoptic Gospels, Jesus—in saying and parable—employed the imagery of wine and weddings to interpret the presence of the Kingdom in his ministry and its fulfillment of all that had gone before.[9]

The evangelist can leave the historical incident unfinished, as he does. He has made his point. Just as the transfer of John's disciples to the company of Jesus signifies the Old giving way to the New, so here is the first of a series of demonstrations of how all religious history finds its summation and interpretation in the coming of Christ. Christ is the key to the meaning of history and faith (cf. Rev. 5:5).

The Mission Begins: The New and the Old (2:13-4:54)

The New Temple (2:13-25). John commences his account of the public ministry of Jesus with a series of scenes which illustrate the difference of the New Order which Jesus inaugurates from the Old. The same theme has already appeared in the call of the first disciples and the first sign at Cana, "title page vignettes" as one scholar terms them, which serve as a preface to his Gospel.

In view of this controlling theological concern it is understandable and appropriate that the author should put the story of the cleansing of the Temple at the very outset of Jesus' work. What more effective contrast could there be between the old revelation and the new than to show how Christ brings to an end the faith centering in the visible Temple of Jerusalem and establishes the faith centering in the invisible Temple of the resurrection community?

The details are familiar enough. Incensed at the desecration of the Temple by the commercialism ostensibly serving pilgrims coming to worship, Jesus scatters the men and the animals with an improvised whip of the kind used for driving cattle. In the Synoptic version he quotes from Jeremiah and Isaiah in his stinging rebuke to the money changers and hucksters for exploiting pilgrims (Matt. 21:13). In John, Jesus accuses them in more general terms of cheapening God's House by making it a public bazaar.

But much more than righteous indignation at the profanation of God's House is involved here, as John sees it. After all, caustic criticism of the corrupt spoils system of the Temple authorities under Roman patronage was common enough within Pharisaic societies and Essene communities of the time.[10] It was a widespread belief among the Jews at this time that God's New Order, once established, would be marked by a new and purified Temple, a gathering place for the righteous from all over the earth.[11] The shocking claim that Jesus makes is that his work marks the dissolution of the old Temple and the imminent establishment of the New, a temple "not made with hands" as his opponents at his trial were to charge him with saying (Mark 14:58).[12]

John the evangelist, to be sure, explains Jesus' words as a cryptic reference to the Resurrection (John 2:21). Perhaps, like Paul, he is thinking of Christ's body as a symbol of the Church, the new People of God who are his true followers. For them surely the true Temple which is the house of prayer for all nations is the new community founded upon the broken body of the Lord raised from the dead and restored to life. The new and greater Temple is the community of the Resurrection![13] In truth "something greater than the temple is here!" (Matt. 12:6)

The New Life (3:1-21). A lively dialogue between a Jewish teacher and Jesus affords new insight into the meaning of this new life found in association with Christ. Nicodemus, a distinguished Jewish teacher and senator in the High Court,[14] seeks a meeting with the Galilean teacher. Perhaps for reasons of privacy and protection of his position, he visits Jesus one evening and engages him in a discussion of the nature of the approaching kingdom of God. In the ensuing conversation, Jesus emphasizes the indispensable condition for man's entrance into the New Order God is establishing. It is a qualification that cannot be met simply by the learned theological discussions carried on in rabbinical schools or by a passive waiting for the catastrophic event to occur. There is no easy stroll into the kingdom of God, nor is it revealed in advance to a privileged minority (Matt. 24:26-28). What is absolutely essential is the realization that it rudely disrupts the old order of things and requires a radical change of life.

The figure Jesus employs is already familiar from our reading of the Synoptic Gospels. "Unless you turn and become like children, you will never enter the kingdom of heaven" (Matt. 18:3). The heavenly birth or birth by the Spirit is an alternate way of emphasizing the necessity for a drastic, thoroughgoing change in the so-called normal way of looking at things, so contrary is the way of the everyday, human world to the world of God.

Half-believing, Nicodemus tries to make light of Jesus' metaphor of change by misunderstanding what he has heard.[15] Birth is a once and for all affair, he argues. But Jesus rejoins with a reminder that the very nature of being human involves several births of which ordinary human existence is primary but preparatory (vs. 6; cf. 1:13). Just as a proselyte to Judaism was baptized in water and just as the followers of John symbolized a fresh start by repenting and receiving baptism, so the child of the Kingdom begins his new existence by the power of the Spirit made available in baptism.

It is the regenerative action of the Holy Spirit, however, beginning from within, which transforms men into new creatures who live close to God, as Ezekiel had anticipated.[16] This is the distinctive meaning and nature of Christian baptism as opposed to the numerous lustration ceremonies of John's day. The new life originates in the joint and indivisible actions of baptism and Pentecost, purification and renewal through water and the Spirit.

It is the man empowered and guided by the invasive Spirit who alone comes to true humanity and is truly free (vs. 8). Life in the Spirit gives to man the glorious liberty of the children of God who are no longer the marionettes of culture, prisoners of the age, as it were. They live *out* of God's world *into* man's world (See Rom. 8:19). Responsible to the first, they are freed from the tyrannies of the second. If the man of the Spirit is truly a free person, it is because the very nature of God's Spirit is to be spontaneous and free. The way we try to "use" God to satisfy our own wishes and purposes more often suggests that we think God is at *our* disposal rather than we at *his!*

From John's point of view and experience, as from ours as latter-day disciples, this renewal of life is immediately available, rather than the distant hope which Rabbi Nicodemus taught and believed.[17] For the kingdom of God was already present in Jesus, and the Community of the Resurrection, the Church, was the sign of its reality in the world.

The only response Nicodemus can make is a stumbling "How?" The full force of the parabolic language of birth and wind has escaped him, as it perhaps escapes so many of us, because he did not really want to hear (John 3:11). Yet there is no experience of the new life apart from an acceptance of the one who speaks these words of life. He is the one whom the Church knows as the Son of man who "descended from heaven" in the Incarnation and who has been "lifted up" in his Ascension (vss. 14-15, cf. 8:28; 12:32-34). He who comes from God and returns to God is the authentic revealer of the things of God; others are only men and no more (vs. 13).[18]

At this point John, the evangelist, seems to move into his own reflection on the meaning of Christ's coming into the world, considered as the double action of love and judgment in God's purpose (3:16-21). Here indeed, as Martin Luther once observed, the whole magnitude of the gospel is epitomized in miniature. Where and why did it all begin? God's costly action in Jesus Christ is explicable only in terms of his amazing love for sinful men and his determination to bring the world not under condemnation but into the freedom of salvation.

That conviction prompts some thoughts on the meaning of judgment. John would be inconsistent with his own religious training and disagree with Scripture if he meant to say that the believer is released from any responsibility in God's judgment. That is not what he means or what he says. The *purpose* of God is unequivocally salvation rather than condemnation. That is sure. And those who come into the new relationship with him are assured that they will never be deemed unworthy and condemned by him. In this sense they are not judged. Apart from God, men live in darkness and that of *their own choosing*. For though they are attracted to the light, the crisis of decision and the demand for total reorganization of their lives leave many of them content to continue in a fantasy world. The believer, on the contrary, is ready and willing to face the demands and moral consequences of coming out of the shadows and beginning to live in the light.[19]

It is characteristic of this Gospel that the opposite of *believing* (note the action word rather than the noun "belief") is not "doubting" but "disobeying" (vs. 36). The truth that is the whole Christian revelation is first and foremost a call to action. That is clear from the unusual expression "he who does what is true" (vs. 21; cf. I John 1:16 K.J.V.). But if the heart of God's truth is the forgiving and saving of men, then "doing the truth" leaves less room for passing judgment upon others than it does for loving them into life. The Christian's proper task is to give respiration, not to deliver death sentences. But the melancholy fact is that men are more ready to pronounce judgment upon other people than they are to help bring them to life.

Interlude: John's Final Testimony (3:22-30). Interrupting the meditation on the theme of the new life is this section on the final witness of John the Baptist.

When Jesus and his disciples returned to work in Judea, the Baptist continued his preaching and baptizing in Samaria at Aenon, some thirty miles north of Jerusalem. A dispute over the significance of baptism leads to another emphatic repudiation of the primacy of John. In language reminiscent of a saying of Jesus repeated by Mark (2:19-20), John the Baptist likens himself to the "best man" in the wedding party rather than the "bridegroom" who is the really important figure (John 3:29).

Further Reflections of the Ministries of John and Jesus (3:30-36). Mention of the Baptist and his work leads to another affirmation of the pre-eminent authority of Christ the Revealer, carrying further the thought of verses 22-30. "He whom God has sent" is a description of Christ which finds repetition some twenty-five times in this Gospel. It virtually becomes a title like "Lamb of God" and "Word." Also the emphasis on sending occurs more than forty times in one form or another! Christ may be mistaken for any man. But to recognize his true identity is to know that he is the Spirit-endowed apostle[20] *par excellence* in whom God speaks to men about matters of life and death. His words are true because he himself is true.

Christ, The Water of Life (4:1-42). If we may think of the Cana miracle, the cleansing of the Temple, and the conversation with Nicodemus as signifying the completion of Judaism by the new revelation in Christ, then the conversation with the

Samaritan woman widens the range of God's revelation and concern for his creatures to include even heretical Judaism. Since the schism in the fourth century between the mixed-blooded Jews (Samaritans) and the full-blooded Jews who returned from Babylon, relationships between the two peoples had been highly strained. Josephus, the Jewish historian who lived in Jesus' time, tells of continuous feuding between them.[21] Rabbi Eliezer ben Hyrcanus reflects the intense feelings after the Second Jewish Revolt (A.D. 132-135) in his words, "He that eats the bread of the Samaritans is like to one that eats the flesh of swine."

Traveling through the district of Samaria on the most direct route to Galilee, Jesus and his disciples paused for refreshment in the midday heat by a famous well which tradition identified with the patriarch Jacob. A woman came out from the nearby village of Sychar (modern 'Askar) to draw water from the well. In several scenes the evangelist sketches a conversation which took place between this anonymous housewife and Jesus (4:7-26); the reaction of the disciples (4:27-38); and the effect on the woman's neighbors who came out to meet him at her insistence (4:39-42).

In a fashion characteristic of this Gospel, John's play on the meaning of familiar words opens up a new insight into the significance of Christ and what he offers to men. Jewish teachers distinguished between storage water kept in a cistern, and spring water which was "living" or running water. Converts to Judaism from the Gentile world were always baptized in "living water." Old Testament writers used the term as a figurative way to describe God's action in restoring life to his people. Jeremiah, for example, laments:

> For my people have committed two evils:
>   they have forsaken me,
> the fountain of living waters,
>   and hewed out cisterns for themselves,
> broken cisterns,
>   that can hold no water.[22]
>
> — *Jeremiah* 2:13

The Torah was often spoken of as living water refreshing the soul.[23] But for John and the new community of faith the real source of living water is found in Jesus Christ. If we compare Jesus' words spoken on another occasion (John 7:38),[24] we discover that John understood this mention of the water of life to be a pictorial designation for the Holy Spirit which purifies and quickens new life in men. He who is singularly endowed with the Spirit bestows that Spirit upon those who are ready and receptive to it.

Jesus' disturbing comment on the woman's private life convinces her that he possesses prophetic power (vs. 19).[25] Now the discussion moves to the Samaritan doctrine of the coming redeemer and the scene of the divine revelation. Here we are at the heart of the drama. Out of their common background with the Jews the Samaritans, too, looked for a savior figure, not the royal Messiah of Israel's hope, but one they called the "Restorer" (*Ta'eb*), based on Moses' prophecy (Deut. 18:15ff.). They accepted only the Torah as canonical Scripture and believed that the God of their fathers appointed Mt. Gerizim not Mt. Zion as the legitimate location for his Temple.

All this is the background of Jesus' self-disclosure as the expected Messiah (John 4:26), and his word that men, when they really know God as Father, will not quarrel with one another over such trivial matters as the place of worship (vs. 21) or the forms of sacrifice. The real question is not *where* but *how* to worship. As spirit, the Father is worshipped in spirit and in truth. This is one of many evidences of the evangelist's concern to show the relationship between church worship and the historical life of Jesus. For him valid worship is not established by impressive pageantry performed in official sanctuaries. Above all, it must be grounded in and tested by the realities of the death and resurrection of Christ.

Christ is forever challenging our institution-centered religion which often debases the Church by making it into a club for religious self-culture. When Christians insist that valid worship takes place only in the local churches of their denomination, Zion and Gerizim have simply been relocated. One of the hopeful features of the modern Church renewal movement is the realization that we are called to honor God's name in the shopping centers of the world as well as the sanctuaries.

With the disciples, who have returned from a visit to the neighboring village to buy food, Jesus shares his enthusiasm for the missionary opportunities presented everywhere they go. "The fields are already white for harvest," he declares joyously. Quoting some proverbs popular among farmers (vss. 35, 37), he tells them that the response they are getting is like that of the sower who has scarcely left the field before the crops begin to ripen for the harvest (vs. 35). It is a time of harvest joy, shared by both sower and reaper, as the New Age begins to be realized among men (vs. 36).[26]

The villagers who come out with their neighbor to meet this strange Jew who condescends to talk about matters of faith with a Samaritan, and a woman at that, listen and come to believe for themselves. "We know that this is indeed the Savior of the world" (vs. 42). This is the point of the whole story to the evangelist. The new faith which centers in Jesus Christ as the true revealer of God to men cannot be bound by previous religious tradition, time, place, national or racial interests. It transcends the parochial differences of Jew and Samaritan, Orthodox, Catholic, and Protestant. It is the good news of God for the *whole world*. In the Word made flesh God is speaking directly and personally to man as man, exposing his darkness and offering the enlightenment of new life.

A Gentile's Faith (4:46-54). It was to a despised alien woman that Jesus made the first admission of his own identity as the Messiah (4:26). Now the second sign John records in which God's glory becomes manifest through Jesus occurs in the healing of a Gentile child. This story has many features in common with an incident involving a Roman imperial officer reported in the Synoptic tradition. It may be a variant account (Matt. 8:5-13 = Luke 7:2-10).

In John's Gospel there is a progressive realization that Christ's words fulfill at once the Temple cult, rabbinic Judaism, and Samaritanism. This incident of the healing of the Gentile child is a symbolic way of carrying that claim still further. Gentile religion, too, is brought to fulfillment in the coming of the universal Savior of men. Whereas Jesus' own Galilean countrymen had seen his deeds in Jerusalem at the Passover feast and still only half-believed or doubted entirely, this man, who was by birth outside the covenant people of Israel, one of the *gōyim* or Gentiles, "believed the word that Jesus spoke to him" (John 4:50).

Christ, The Lord of the Sabbath (5:1-47)

In the other accounts of the historical mission of Jesus, we can read in considerable detail about the conflict between Jesus and the official interpreters of Judaism which increased as his work gathered momentum. Debates and clashes took place over such matters as his free association with persons of dubious reputation, his healing of the sick, his unconventionally liberal attitude to practices of ritual handwashing, fasting, and other ritual laws of purity. A principal point of offense in Jesus' conduct was his attitude toward the laws guarding the Sabbath from profanation. A reflection of the Sabbath controversy appears in this story of the healing of a chronic invalid.

Breaking the sequence of Galilean episodes, this Jerusalem story is set at an ancient Lourdes, probably located in a suburb called "New City." The place name varies in the manuscript tradition. The earliest form of the text may have read "There is in Jerusalem, by the Sheep Pool [a place] called in Aramaic Bethesda (or Bethsaida) having five porches." This building, popularly called "Five Porches," probably located near the spot occupied later by the basilica church of St. Anne in the northeast section of the city, was a favorite haunt of invalids who hoped to be cured by the miraculous action of the pool waters.

The first scene (vss. 1-9) presents the basic narrative. There are deep implications in Jesus' apparently simple question to the invalid, "Do you want to be healed?" (vs. 6) What an absurd question to put to a man who had been ill for thirty-eight years! But not so absurd on second thought when we realize how, under the cover of complaint, some people enjoy illness. Was this a man who nursed ill health, clinging to his sickness as a way of life without actually realizing it? In any event Jesus' searching word brings to him new strength and the recovery of health.

It is obvious that John intends a deeper meaning for health than effective physical functioning. Full health in this Gospel like healing in the other Gospels must always be understood in the sense of a *wholeness of personality,* including *physical, emotional and spiritual* soundness. This is just what the New Testament word translated "salvation" really signifies. It is the care of bodies as well as the care and cure of souls. Indeed the ensuing discussion shows that there were spiritual concomitants to this man's illness (vs. 14). But though guilt was recognized as a contributory factor, it is important to note that neither here nor elsewhere does Jesus endorse the popular Jewish diagnosis of sickness as the necessary consequence of sin (cf. 9:3; 11:4).

In the second scene of the little drama (vss. 10-18), a discussion develops over the whole question of healing on the Sabbath day. Since healing for Jesus is a part of the whole act of rescuing human life, it is an expression of God's continuing work of salvation. Hence its validity as a demonstration of the divine purpose, whether performed on the Sabbath or any other day, cannot be brought to question. When men are being brought out of shadowy, partial existence into the light of true existence, then the name of God is truly hallowed and adored. Indeed acts of prayer and worship which shut the doors of our churches against the cries of human need constitute the real desecration of the Sabbath. "Leave your gift there before the altar and go; first be reconciled to your brother . . ." (Matt. 5:24). The God of the Bible is not a drone but a worker God who calls men to share in a ceaseless redemptive labor that cannot be regulated by human calendars. For the man of faith this is the real "right to work."

But this theological consideration already leads us into the third and final scene (vss. 19-47). What is the relationship between the one Sent and the Sender? In what does the authority of Jesus to represent the Father consist? We can hear echoes here of questions put by the converts in their confirmation instructions in the Church of John's day, or even the accusations of Jewish and Roman critics of the Christian faith. What, for example, is the relation of the Christian Sunday to the Jewish Sabbath? The healing is incidental to John's interest in these questions.

In words of Christ which may reflect the preaching of the early church, we hear that the common work of the Son and the Father does not mean the independent parallel activity of one who makes "himself equal with God." Rather in the Old Testament sense of sonship as divine appointment and obedient response, the work of the Son is dependent upon and expressive of the redemptive concern of the Father who has sent him. The words and works of the Son are one with the words and works of the Father. This is the real reason why Christ stirs up such dissent and divided reaction wherever he goes. The real challenge he presents is whether men can and will perceive in him the Father's call to move out of death into life. It is because of who he is and what they are that men react to him in violent extremes of love and hate.

There was a common enough belief among the Jewish people that God would raise the dead on the Last Day. Jesus refers also to the doctrine that the heavenly Son of man who was to come would be involved in that future Resurrection and Judgment. But the shocking claim of Jesus is that the last things *are already happening* in his ministry. "The hour is coming, and now is." The spiritually dead are now hearing the voice of the Son of God and finding resurrection to life.

> In very truth, anyone who gives heed to what I say and puts his trust in him who sent me *has hold of eternal life,* and does not come up for judgment, *but has already passed from death to life.*[27]
>
> — *John* 5:24, N.E.B.

This is what men stumble over, yesterday *and* today. We may admit that God *some* day will give his people new life, no doubt, beyond the grave. It is a popular expectation. But can we see that he is even *now* raising the dead and giving them new life through his Son? And recognizing this, are we willing to accept this new life ourselves? That takes more than theological speculations about a future which is not yet real to us and hence does not affect us where we live. It means to turn and face the One who comes to us today with the promise of life now.

Taking on the atmosphere of a court of law, the discourse concludes with an enumeration of converging witnesses to the authority of Christ as the revealer of the life of God to men (vss. 30-44). In Deuteronomy 19:15 it is said that the establishment of a testimony requires the support of at least two witnesses. Four are presented here. To those who can really discern what is going on, it ought to be apparent that Jesus fulfills the testimony of John the Baptist about the Coming One (vss. 33-36a). The whole of Jesus' ministry in action ought to bear convincing evidence to the honest observer that he is the one come from the Father to give men life (vs. 36b; cf. 10:25, 38; 14:11). The "signs" Jesus performs disclose to the eye of faith the one who himself is the true sign. The real miracle, in other words, consists in no single act; it is Jesus himself who is the true sign of God's presence and activity in the world (see Luke 11:30). It is the Father himself who bears witness ultimately to him (vss. 32, 37-38). If anyone really and truly "hears" Jesus' words and "sees" his works, he must confess that it is the Father himself speaking and acting in them.

Finally, the Scriptures themselves, the pride and joy of his critics, make their witness to him (vss. 39-47). One may know all the words of Scripture and fail to recognize the Word. But the real purpose of the Bible is not to present men with a catalogued system of ethical and religious truth to be venerated as the absolute Word of God. It is instead to mark the crossroads where man and God meet each other. So Martin Luther insisted that Christ is to be acknowledged as the Lord and King of Scripture. When we understand them aright, these sacred writings, like John the Baptist, point us to him who alone is the true and living Word. "Behold, the Lamb of God."

> O Word of God incarnate,
> O Wisdom from on high,
> O Truth unchanged, unchanging,
> O Light of our dark sky:
> We praise Thee for the radiance
> That from the hallowed page,
> A lantern to our footsteps,
> Shines on from age to age.[28]
> — William W. How

Christ, the Bread of Life (6:1-71)

The Gospel of John contains its own version of the story of the Loaves and the Fishes so familiar to us from the Synoptic tradition (vss. 1-15). One cannot be sure whether John's account is based on the latter, or whether each is indebted to a common source. In any event, it is evident soon enough that our writer is concerned with more than the details of a lakeside meal at which a hungry multitude was miraculously fed. As we soon see, the historical story becomes the basis for a parabolic interpretation of Jesus as the bread of life for humanity. At one point Jesus rebukes the eager crowd for looking for a food supply close at hand rather than discerning the real sign behind the meal they have enjoyed together (vs. 26), (though some present did have a partial understanding [vs. 14]). So the meal becomes the fourth of the seven signs dealt with in this Gospel.

The story as it is told by the evangelist clearly has messianic implications. That the hunger of the crowd was satisfied by this distribution of a lad's few barley loaves and fishes was something beyond a marvelous feat of power. John adds a very important detail unmentioned by the other Gospel writers. Some of the people began to say that Jesus might be the prophet foretold long ago by the blessed Moses himself, the prophet of the last times some had taken the Baptist to be (1:21, 25). "This is indeed the prophet who is to come into the world!" (6:14) Some sort of an abortive messianic demonstration took place spontaneously; as a result Jesus was forced to slip away and find privacy in the hills (vs. 15).[29]

In a sequence identical with the Synoptics, the lakeside meal is followed by a narrative about the recrossing of the Sea of Galilee (vss. 16-21). This fifth of the seven signs is probably told for the same purpose as the others: a parable of Christ's significance for mankind, but the writer does not elaborate upon this sign. In any event the words, "It is I; do not be afraid," have brought comfort to many a storm-tossed disciple through the centuries whose fear was dissipated by the assurance of the Lord's presence in the midst of peril. Christ is the one who brings our little craft through the storm to safe harbor.

> Then they were glad because they had quiet,
> and he brought them to their desired haven.
> — *Psalms* 107:30

The remainder of this chapter is given to an exposition of the inner meaning of the story in verses 1-5 which one scholar has termed the "Galilean Lord's Supper." We may consider its message in two parts: 1, verses 27-47, on the person of Christ as the living bread; and 2, verses 48-65, on the bread of the Lord's Supper. [30] Notice particularly the progressive narrowing of the circles of the audience as the discourse develops. At first, the multitude constitutes the body of the hearers. As the teaching becomes more difficult to understand and to accept, the group thins out to the disciples. Not all of them can agree with him, however; some turn away (vss. 60, 66). Finally only the twelve remain (vs. 67), the nucleus of the new community of faith.

1. The scene is set in a synagogue at Capernaum (vss. 24, 59). Despite what has happened, the people who gather to hear him call for some external proof that will authenticate his claim that he is the one sent to them from God. They clamor for something comparable to the manna which once saved their fathers from starvation in the wilderness (vss. 30-31). Appealing to a popular understanding of the New Age as economic security, they are fascinated by the notion of a bread-providing Messiah. "At

that time," one apocalyptist had predicted, "supplies of manna will fall on the earth. Then shall they eat therefrom, for it will be the end of time" (*II Baruch* 29:8). It could be said of them, as of the Roman official whose son Jesus cured, "Unless you see signs and wonders you will not believe" (4:48).

In reply Jesus promptly corrects them. That manna was not the real bread of heaven at all. The bread which is God's gift to men is not supplied to satisfy the hunger of stomachs, though that is a basic need to be met. What matters most of all is a food that nourishes the inner man and makes genuine life possible. In the words of D. T. Niles,

> The desperate need of men is not for bread alone — though all men are hungry for bread; it is for the word of God which will make their bread holy bread.[31]

What this heavenly food may be is now identified. "I am the bread of life" (vs. 35). Here is the first of another series of seven great affirmations made in this Gospel. In words representing the message of the exalted Christ to his Church and verified in Christian experience, Jesus is identified as bread (6:35, 48, 51); light (8:12); the door (10:7, 9); the good shepherd (10:11, 14); resurrection and life (11:25); the way, the truth, the life (14:6); and the vine (15:1, 5).

2. In the second section (vss. 48-65) we can hear overtones of the observance of the Lord's Supper in the Church. The evangelist understands the words

of Jesus as interpretive of the inner meaning of this fellowship ritual in Christian worship. Hints of that are already given in the reference to the Passover season in verse 4 and the giving of thanks in verse 11. But the mention of both eating and drinking in verses 53-56 seems to refer directly to this sacramental act in the Church. "Flesh and blood" means the whole life of the Son of God given for the life of the world.

John believes that the act of worship begins in faith, is supported by faith, and culminates in a deepened faith. To those who want to convert the symbols of flesh and blood into substances of magical power, he insists that it is the *words* of the spirit-filled Christ heard in faith that are life-giving. "It is the spirit that gives life, the flesh is of no avail; the words that I have spoken to you are spirit and life" (6:63; cf. 3:5-6, 8). Word and sacrament belong together for John; too often we separate them as though preaching were something quite different from the Lord's Supper and both, from baptism. One of our most familiar hymns of the Holy Communion teaches us that word and sacrament are twin forms of a total act which is the subject of the Christian's gratitude:

> For the bread, which thou hast broken,
> For the wine, which thou hast poured,
> For the words, which thou hast spoken,
> Now we give thee thanks, O, Lord.[32]
>   — Louis F. Benson

It is not without reason that John was called the Liturgist by the later Church fathers and that medieval art depicted him as the greatest interpreter of the sacraments, picturing him holding the communion cup.

But this teaching is too strong for some of the disciples. Perhaps John is thinking of some of the followers of the Lord in his own day who doubted that the heavenly Lord could actually have assumed the limitations of human existence. They found offensive the emphasis on the reality of the Incarnation which is expressed here and elsewhere in this Gospel by the words "flesh and blood." They "drew back" (vs. 66). The twelve remain and swear their undying loyalty to him. Peter voices their decision in the Johannine equivalent to the confession at Caesarea Philippi. "Lord, to whom shall we go? You have the words of eternal life; and we have believed, and have come to know, that you are the Holy One of God" (vs. 69).

Jesus himself and his whole mission among men is the life-sustaining bread given to the world. The crowds want him to give them some*thing*, some blessing, some benefit. He gives them some*one*: himself. This is his gift and we are still trying to decide whether to be pleased or disappointed.

Chapter FOUR

Coming to Life

> Unreal City,
> Under the brown fog of a winter dawn,
> A crowd flowed over London Bridge, so many,
> I had not thought death had undone so many.[1]

THESE LINES of T. S. Eliot written about contemporary life in a modern metropolis remind us again how closely the drive to life and the nearness of death are intertwined. Jesus interprets the cheerful sadness that pervades much human living as the condition of man in his tragic isolation from the Father God. It is death, both self-chosen and inescapable, which holds dominion over man's life, however much be boasts of his freedom to enjoy the good life.

Christ is the great Life-bringer. That is the heart and center of John's witness to Jesus Christ. In a fast-moving sequence of vivid word-pictures this truth is presented in parabolic language. Four word-pictures appear in the central section of his Gospel (7:37 - 10:39), symbols of the meaning of Christ for man's life in the world. Two of them are already familiar to us; the other two are new.

FOUR IMAGES:
Water, Light, Door, Shepherd (7:1-10:39)

The discourses of Jesus in which these symbols appear are set in the context of the Jewish festival of Sukkoth or Tabernacles, the most popular of all the Jewish feasts. To get the full impact of these words we need to refresh our memories about this great eight day autumn feast,[2] and especially to read the passage from the prophecy of Zechariah which is the special lesson or *Haphtarah* read at this time (Zech. 14).

Opening the ceremonies that were regarded as a foreshadowing of the Day of the Lord, there was, in the Court of the Women, a great illumination said to be reflected in every courtyard in the city. On each of the seven days, moreover, water drawn from the famous pool of Siloam was poured out as a libation in the Temple. Had not the prophet said:

> On that day there shall be neither cold nor frost. And there shall be continuous day (it is known to the Lord), not day and not night, for at evening time there shall be light. On that day living waters shall flow out from Jerusalem. . . .   — *Zechariah* 14:6-8

As the golden pitcher of water was carried in procession up to the Temple, the words of Isaiah were recited: "With joy you will draw water from the wells of salvation" (Isa. 12:3). Water and light—ancient religious symbols for the creative energy of God which quickens all living things and introduces man to that reality which is called eternal life.

Jesus had gone from Galilee to the festival in Jerusalem after spurning his brothers' sarcastic suggestion that he put on a public display in the capital city to gain some new recruits to replace those he had lost at home (7:1-10). Long ago he had decided against the use of any kind of messianic demonstration as popularly conceived at the time. As a result, his ministry continued to provoke divided reactions among the people (vss. 11-13).

The River of Life (7:14-52). It is in the midst of this popular celebration that Jesus begins to teach openly near the Treasury in the Temple area. Appealing to the familiar imagery of the ceremonial water, he proclaims,

> "If any one is thirsty let him come to me; whoever believes in me, let him drink." As Scripture says, "Streams of living water shall flow out from within him." [3]
> — *John* 7:37, 38, N.E.B.

It is the voice of the new community of faith celebrating with joy its experience of the risen Lord whose presence and transforming power are realized in its midst. As life-giving Spirit he is the source and the transmitter of life to his people (vs. 39). This is what the death and resurrection of Jesus meant to the early church. The regenerative Spirit was the gift of the risen Lord to his people.

It is inevitable that Christ's words should precipitate a controversy (vss. 15-24). Wherever he goes, whatever he does in this Gospel, he becomes the great divider of men. Alluding to the earlier question about Sabbath observance, Jesus reminds his critics that even the Law of Moses permits the ceremony of initiation of a convert into Judaism to take precedence over the Sabbath prohibition of work in any form. His skill in rabbinical debate elicits bewildered admiration from the audience.

Earlier when the question was raised as to what the works of God are which the devout man should be doing (6:28), Jesus declared that the divine demand is met when a man accepts with his whole heart the messenger from God (6:29). Here again we learn, "If any man's will is to do his [God's] will, he shall know whether the teaching is from God or whether I am speaking on my own authority" (7:17).

As the controversy between Jesus and the Jews intensifies, some of the bystanders begin to ask whether he may not indeed be the expected Messiah (vss. 25-31). A popular belief about the Coming One assumed that he might be present among his people incognito before suddenly displaying himself in his true colors. Since it is generally known that this teacher is from somewhere in Galilee, and not from Bethlehem, he is evidently disqualified (vss. 41-42, 52). Others half believe. Priestly authorities and Pharisees or "Associates," as they preferred to be called, speak with scorn of the peasantry's opinions and ridicule one of their own number, the learned Nicodemus, for his cautious attitude. "Are you from

Galilee too? Search and you will see that the prophet[4] is not to rise from Galilee" (vs. 52). Their blithe assurance that any legitimate leader must first win the endorsement of the academic and ecclesiastical community is a fallacy repeated numberless times in history. This was only another striking instance. Truth, no respecter of persons, may be repulsed by the sophisticated and find hospitality among the commoners.

The Fifth Freedom (8:12-59). Now calling attention to the other major symbol of the ceremony, Jesus declares, "I am the light of the world; he who follows me will not walk in darkness, but will have the light of life" (vs. 12).[5] With a characteristic play on words, the evangelist represents Jesus taking up the question of the hidden Messiah to elaborate it into a problem fundamental to the whole human quest. They think they know where he "comes from." Actually the tragedy is that they do not. Their conversation about origins centers in genealogy and geography: Galilee and Bethlehem. "I know whence I have come and whither I am going, but you do not know whence I come or whither I am going" (vs. 14). If they did they would know he comes from the Father and returns to the Father.

Here are the basic issues that confront every thoughtful person. *Who* am I? *Where* have I come from? *What* is my destiny? In Jesus Christ, this Gospel affirms, those questions find their answer. To know him is to begin to understand the meaning, purpose, and possibilities of one's own life. Apart from that understanding, a person never comes into full realization of his essential humanity. The light Christ sheds upon the mystery of our being reveals to us the possibility that we may indeed be reborn into newness of life as sons of God.

When man understands fully his divine origin and destiny, he can, in obedience to his Maker, become a new kind of person—at once free and responsible. His world begins to assume integrity and come together as a whole. He realizes with a gasp of surprise that he is not really an excrescense of society, conditioned, and controlled by this honky-tonk, papier-mâché world in which he is so deeply involved. God is in his beginning and in his ending. He comes *into* this world, not *out* of it, and he can be the bearer of unfettered spirit which has a richness and strength because it is generated by and established in God himself.

The question of who this Jesus of Nazareth is remains to be settled (vss. 21-59). For John this is *the* fundamental challenge of the gospel, the answer to which is of momentous consequence for humankind everywhere. Admittedly it is his tragic death on the cross and his glorification in heaven which will most clearly reveal his true nature and authority (vs. 28; cf. 6:62). But John knows that even that decisive event cannot *coerce* men into believing that Christ comes from God and shares his very nature, signified by the divine name "I am."[6] Some will scoff and turn away; others will yield and pray.

The dialogue continues with some Jews who are said to believe him but who obviously only do so in a fitful inquiring way, for they soon reveal their skepticism and draw his rebuke (31ff.). They remind us of the halfhearted disciples pictured in 6:60, 66 who found his teaching more than they could take and resigned from his company. In this exchange between Christ and his critics the basic issues of freedom and slavery, heritage and sonship are explored.

What does it mean to be a free person? Those who are deprived of the franchise understandably believe that there is no freedom apart from political liberty. But even in a democratic state one can be controlled by patterns of culture or hemmed in by pervasive social customs so that one's personal freedom is highly questionable. And what shall be said about the dominant attitudes and driving compulsions, the loves and the resentments which often plague us so that with Paul we have to admit, "I do not understand my own actions. For I do not do what I want, but I do the very thing I hate" (Rom. 7:15). Who, then, is really free?

Jesus' well-known word on freedom in 31-32 has been used in support of everything from a liberal editorial policy to a mental health program. But what he really meant must emerge out of a study of the saying in its total context. Slavery, according to verse 34, is slavery to sin and its consequence of death (vs. 51). Sin, in this Gospel, is primarily understood, not as a moral infraction, but as disbelief, the willful rejection of Christ, man's stubborn refusal to permit the word of life in Christ to find access into his life. It is the whole Christian revelation, the gospel, which exercises a liberating power, freeing imprisoned minds and hearts. The vitalizing energy of the gospel is imparted as a gift, but it is a gift with strings attached, a gift which becomes available to perform its work of freedom only insofar as one remains loyal to the commands of Jesus (vs. 32b). So the practical outcome of disbelief is disobedience (3:36). Conversely, it is in the course of continuing faithful discipleship that the gospel delivers us from bondage into the glorious freedom of the sons of God.[7] Christian freedom, it turns out, is both a gift to be accepted and an achievement to be earned.

Human pride always resists any accusations against personal independence. The immediate response to all this talk of slavery and freedom is the haughty claim to a heritage of freedom which is inalienable. "We are descendants of Abraham, and have never been in bondage to anyone" (vs. 8:33). That has an uncomfortably familiar ring to it. It is ironical that often those who have less claim to freedom are loudest in their boasts that they possess it. Some people imagine they are free, someone has said, when they are really only unbuttoned!

But true freedom, won at bitter cost, is not simply to become a form of social inheritance like a patrimony. Nor is true sonship simply a matter of the operation of the Mendelian laws of heredity. "If you were Abraham's children, you would do what Abraham did" (vs. 39b).[8] The behavior of these "descendants of Abraham" toward Christ is proof enough that they are not friends of God but of his Adversary! True freedom does not mean subjective arbitrariness but being a real, responsible person.

On hearing this denunciation, his listeners seek to stone him—they resort to violence, the customary recourse of those who cannot meet the truth in arguments! Earlier they had used the smear technique (vs. 48); now it was brute force (vs. 59). But for the time being Jesus escaped their hands.

Corrected Vision (9:1-41). The same theme of light and darkness begun in 8:12 is presented again in chapter 9 in the form of a concrete illustration, in the story of the healing of a man who was a victim of congenital blindness. Stories of blindness healed also occur in the other Gospels. The concern of this evangelist is to make clear that these acts of Jesus are symbolic of his total ministry to men dwelling in darkness, men who need to be guided into the light of understanding. Seeing is of several sorts. It is optical recognition; it is also the purity of heart which beholds God (Matt. 5:8). One man's journey out of darkness into light is here set forth in a series of dramatic scenes. Washing in the waters of Siloam after Jesus treated his eyes, the blind man recovers his sight. As verse 7 makes clear, the evangelist intends this as an allegory of the ministry of Christ who is often spoken of as the one whom God Sent.[9] He may have been thinking especially of the regenerative work of the Spirit in the act of baptism, for this was sometimes spoken of as *enlightenment* (Heb. 6:4).

At first there is only a partial spiritual sight: "The man called Jesus" told him what to do (John 9:11, 15). A higher level of vision is reached when, in response to repeated badgering by the Pharisees, the poor fellow declares, "He is a prophet" (vs. 17). His faith ripens in the heated exchange and, at the call to forthright confession in the presence of hostile inquisitors, full "sight" becomes a reality. "Lord, I believe" (vs. 38).

All the tragedy of our human situation is exposed in the next few statements of Jesus (vss. 39-41). Here is the pity: that men who pride themselves on their unclouded vision often are badly in need of corrective lenses. Yet they stubbornly insist that they see everything in clear perspective. So they must accept responsibility for their condition. "Now that you say, 'We see' your guilt remains" (vs. 41).[10] Now we know who the man is who was born blind: he is Everyman. What kind of sight is it that turns blind eyes to human need? How much better to be like this sightless beggar and receive sight, rather than like the blind leaders who are oblivious to their sorry condition. "The real atheists," writes Alan Richardson, "are not those troubled by honest doubt but those who trust in their own righteousness."[11]

The Flock of Christ (10:1-21). This central section

of the Gospel of John, chapters 7 through 10, with its four pictures of Christ, as the water, the light, the door, the shepherd, comes to a close with a symbolical discourse on the nature and work of Christ (10:1-21) followed by an exposition (vss. 22-42). We may speak of this as a parable-allegory of the Shepherd and the Door, since Christ uses both these metaphors, combining features of both types of pictorial thought.

Both images are characteristic of biblical language. David was described as the shepherd-ruler of his nation (e.g. Ps. 78:70-72). Moses, too, was described in pastoral language as shepherding a flock (e.g. Isa. 63:11). But primarily for Israel it was the God Yahweh who was the true shepherd of his people, portrayed unforgettably in the beloved Shepherd psalm (Ps. 23). In the New Testament it is Christ, himself, who is identified as the Good Shepherd, a depiction which, because of its Hebrew and pagan usages, endeared itself to early Christians. Literature and catacomb art attest to that.[12]

The parable speaks in acid criticism of false shepherds, hirelings and brigands, in terms which remind us of similar prophetic indictments of incompetent leadership.[13] It is useless to try to identify them with historical persons. Probably John has in mind both bogus messiahs and some of the more headstrong leaders of the church in his own day who fulfill the warning words of the Lord, "Beware of false prophets, who come to you in sheep's clothing but inwardly are ravenous wolves" (Matt. 7:15; cf. Mark 13: 21-22, etc.).

Before and since Christ there have been self-styled revealers who, in fact, have been imposters and charlatans, John means to say. Society is never without its messianic pretenders and salvation hucksters. Only Christ is the Good Shepherd. He alone will lay down his life for the sheep, and this he does willingly and gladly, for his only concern is their welfare. The true leader must share that spirit of sacrificial service, concerned for the welfare of those in his care rather than for his own personal safety or prestige.

Alternating with this appealing figure, particularly meaningful to a people living in a simple pastoral society, is another. To speak of Christ as the Door to the sheepfold (John 10:9; cf. vs. 7) may seem strange until we are reminded that this, too, is a familiar word picture in Jewish literature. (The portal marking the entrance to heaven is mentioned in Jacob's dream [Gen. 28:17] and in Psalm 78:23. A Jewish apocryphal writing of the second century B.C. preserved in Aramaic and Greek speaks of the messianic high priest who will open the "gates of paradise" [*Test. of Levi* 18:10].) It is also a striking way of describing the gathering of the People of God—the Church—within the security of this fold—under Christ's protection.

But we need to note that the door is a means of exit as well as entrance. The sheep go in and they go out (vs. 9). The church whose doors only open inward and not outward will become a ghetto, a refuge from the world rather than an entrance into it. The People of God must not only be called together into the community of the Church, relatively protected from the noises and dangers of the world; they must also be involved in society *where the Good Shepherd is at work.*

The whole missionary imperative of the Church of Christ the Shepherd is compressed within the statement of verse 16. There are other sheep in other folds, not simply the believing Jews in the community of Israel. In the communities of the nations there are those who are to respond to his shepherd call and gather about him. But there is not the slightest suggestion here of national-cultural communities, coexisting in segregated groups. There is to be only one flock, just as there is a single Shepherd! Nor, to carry out the figure to absurdity, do the members of the flock choose their companions. It is the Shepherd who calls and it is the Shepherd who brings them together in the fold and scatters them again out in the pasture.

The Father and The Son (10:22-39). The scene shifts from Sukkoth to Hanukkah,[14] but the principal themes which began with chapter seven continue. Again the bold claim: I am from the Father who is present in me. Again the angry response, this time an accusation of blasphemy, a religious crime punishable by death according to the law of the land.[15] In reply Jesus asks his accusers how they interpret a passage in the very Book they hold inspired and authoritative. In Psalm 82:6 Israel herself, blessed as the recipient of the Law at Sinai, is addressed as divine. Is that blasphemy, too?

But the true identity of this Galilean teacher is not established in the last analysis by ingenious prooftexting or any kind of formal argument. It is his whole ministry that must provide the evidence. To those who are ready and willing to see, the works of Jesus are explainable as the works of God (vss. 25, 38).[16] They recognize that God and his salvation are present in him affecting the lives of men. This recognition can only lead to the conclusion that he is the Father's representative, the true messenger who comes from God to bring the word of life to man. "I give them eternal life" (vs. 28).

Christ the Resurrection and the Life (10:40-11:44)

Leaving the city, Jesus returns to Perean Bethany, the earlier scene of John's preaching and the beginning of his own ministry (vs. 40). It is here presumably that he receives news of the serious illness and death of a dear friend who lived in Judean Bethany near Jerusalem.

Lazarus' restoration to life by the act of Jesus becomes the seventh of the signs which the evangelist has singled out for recital and interpretation. In keeping with his dominant intention to show that every scene and every saying of Jesus is incandescent with the heavenly glory, John here centers his attention on what this incident reveals about Jesus as the realization of the resurrection and its life. There are thematic echoes of a parable Jesus once told about an anonymous rich man, a beggar named Lazarus, and the issues of life, death, and resurrection (Luke 16:19-31).

It is evident that the focus of interest here is no more the resuscitation of a dead man than "diseases of the eye" is the central point of chapter nine. Eventually Lazarus had to meet the same fate that faces everyone. What purpose then was served by this reprieve from the sentence of death? It would be foreign to the total presentation of Jesus in the Gospels to reduce the story of Lazarus to a dazzling display of supernatural power for self-glorification. Indeed, as Jesus' parable of the Rich Man and the Beggar makes clear, men who will not believe the word of God are not likely to be convinced by miraculous displays (Luke 16:31).

If we recognize in the story of Lazarus a parable of how Christ brings indestructible life to men, we find the Christian message which the evangelist intended. The historical details in the story of the Blind Beggar and the story of Lazarus are subordinated to the larger purpose of theological truth. When does one learn to see? In company with Christ. Where does one begin to wake up and live? In company with Christ. In this Gospel death, like sleep and darkness, is a symbol of misfortune, judgment, alienation—all that separates man from God. Coming to life means escape from isolation and negation and to enter into creative fellowship with God. "Death" is living a spurious existence which results from the folly and vanity of the world. "Life" is living a genuine existence which comes from the truth and goodness of God.

Essential to any interpretation of the story of Lazarus are such words of Jesus as we have read in chapter five:

> Truly, truly I say to you, the hour is coming, and *now is*, when the dead will hear the voice of the Son of God, and those who hear will live. — *John* 5:25
> Truly, truly, I say to you, he who hears my word and believes him who sent me, has eternal life; he does not come into judgment, but *has passed from death to life.* — *John* 5:24

Christ enters into the very regions of death where men are trapped to lead them into freedom and life. The double event of Good Friday and Easter, life made available through the self-offering of the Son, is prefigured in this story of how Lazarus was brought from death to life. It is clear from Thomas' first reaction to the news of Lazarus' death—his premonition that a return to Bethany would bring about Jesus' death—that John views this incident as a preparation for the Passion story (vss. 7-8,16).

Whereas this particular story shows that Jesus felt and shared human suffering (vss. 34-35), Lazarus was already dead before Jesus left Perea. Perhaps Jesus' delay in responding to the news of his illness (vs. 6) is best understood as expressive of his sovereign independence from all human claims and demands which is displayed elsewhere in this Gospel (see 2:3f.; 7:3-9). The Christ of the Fourth Gospel is not to respond to man's beck and call, nor to be fitted into *human plans and programs.* Christ is not to be confused with the genie of Aladdin's lamp! Coming to the village of Bethany, Jesus and his companions learn that their friend had died four days earlier. Since according to Jewish belief all hope of revival from the sleep of death ended after the third day, this mention of the time elapsed emphasizes the fact that all vestiges of life had departed from the body.

We cannot penetrate the mystery deeply enough to know all that actually happened. But at the commanding word of Jesus, "Lazarus, come out," death released its claim and Lazarus was restored to life.

This much is sure. Whatever happened to Lazarus was in John's opinion a symbol of what could happen to bring men everywhere out of spiritual death into real life. The center of the whole piece can be identified in the extraordinary words the Master spoke to grieving Martha. "I am the resurrection and the life; he who believes in me, though he die, yet shall he live, and whoever lives and believes in me shall never die" (vss. 25-26). Where Christ is present there can be no death, only life. He is God's victor over man's greatest enemy. In anticipation of our coming to complete life beyond this world, there is available here and now the chance to come alive.

The question to Martha is the question the evangelist would address to us all: "Do you believe this?"

Official Intervention (11:45-54)

The consequence of this seventh sign is a decision reached by the Supreme Council or Sanhedrin to arrest the Galilean and sentence him to death. In the Synoptic Gospels the cleansing of the Temple at the opening of the final week provokes the authorities to seal Jesus' fate. As we have seen (2:14-17), John places the cleansing of the Temple at the beginning of Christ's ministry. He predates the decision of the Supreme Council, associating it with the raising of Lazarus, the sign of the Resurrection. In this Gospel the death of Jesus is the consequence of his gift of life to Lazarus. In giving life to others, he himself dies.

A striking instance of what has been called "Johannine irony" is presented in the statement of the ruling high priest Joseph Caiaphas. What appears to be a common sense proposal for averting the unwelcome intervention of the Roman governor is couched in the form of a prophecy about the real significance of Jesus' death. "It is expedient for you that one man should die for the people, and that the whole nation should not perish" (vs. 50).[17] Temporarily avoiding arrest, Jesus and his disciples retire into the privacy of a little northern Judean village called Ephraim near Bethel where they remain until the approach of the freedom festival of Passover (vs. 54).

A Symbolic Anointing (11:55-12:11)

As the Passover festival approached, Jesus returned to the capital city for the last time. Visiting in the home of his friends Mary, Martha, and Lazarus in Bethany, a few miles outside of Jerusalem, Jesus is the recipient of a spontaneous act of affection which John views as deeply symbolical of the coming events. It is difficult to determine the relationship between the three stories of the anointing of Jesus mentioned in the Gospels.[18] It looks as though John combined the two accounts in Mark and Luke's writings of the gospel history, identifying the unnamed woman as the sister of Lazarus.[19] A sharp contrast in character types is presented by Mary and Judas Iscariot in this scene. The one in grateful devotion to her beloved Teacher chose a very expensive oil for this Oriental act of anointing. The other thinly disguised his personal avarice under a veneer of pseudo-humanitarianism. Jesus' own comment is more obscure in the Johannine version than in the Synoptics. The Greek sentence seems to mean that Mary's act of devotion is an unconscious anticipation of his coming death and burial. "Let her alone, let her keep it for the day of my burial" (vs. 7). Perhaps, too, the evangelist interpreted it as the anointing of Jesus as the King-Messiah who will now move toward assassination. The stage is set for the final drama.

King for a Day (12:12-19)

John follows the traditional account of the entry of Jesus into the Holy City. However, he heightens the symbolism, presenting Jesus as a kingly victor. At the Sukkoth festival, the joyful pilgrims waved *lulabs,* made of myrtle and willow branches with a spray of palm leaves, emblems of victory and salvation (see Rev. 7:9f.). Adapting the Hallel psalm chanted in the ceremony, the crowd from the city, attracted by the notoriety of the sign worker from Galilee, cried aloud:

> *Hoshianna!* [Save us!]
> Blessed is he who comes in the name of the
> Lord,[20] even the King of Israel.

John implicitly interprets the entry as a fulfillment of the messianic prophecy in Zechariah 9:9. The early Christian church certainly understood the demonstration as a messianic ovation on the part of the crowd. But the language is ambiguous. The Passover psalm refers to the worshippers who are blessed, and in Israel God himself is the great King. We cannot be sure in what sense, if any, the people in this spontaneous ovation hailed Jesus as the messianic king. One thing is sure: they failed to comprehend what Jesus understood messiahship to mean. Do we? Testimonials are impressive but ephemeral things. Jesus' haunting word spoken on another occasion cannot be put aside, "Why do you call me 'Lord, Lord,' and not do what I tell you?" (Luke 6:46)

The Cross and Mission (12:20-26)

With the approach of some Greeks who ask to see Jesus, the writer of the Gospel sees the public ministry coming to its climax. The witness of God's gift of life to the world beyond Judaism is the missionary outcome of Jesus' death and exaltation. These visitors anticipate the decisive events which in fact will project the mission into the empire. A new note is added to Jesus' words. No longer does he speak of his hour yet to come. From now on he can say, "The hour *has come* for the Son of man to be glorified" (vs. 23).[21]

In a singular and emphatic way this Gospel insists that the tragic fact of the death of Christ, when seen in the perspective of faith in God's saving purpose, is not tragedy at all but the return and enthronement of the Son of God in glory (3:14; 6:62; 8:28; 12:23-36). The cross is for the healing of the nations. It will not stay put on Hangman's Hill outside the walls of Jerusalem. It breaks through the national barriers of Judaism and begins a march into the wider world beyond. With brilliant insight John teaches us that (in spite of its horror) a true understanding of the cross recognizes in it the glorification of Jesus as heavenly Lord and the missionary commission of Christ and his Church.

The Agony and the Ecstasy (12:27-36)

The realization that the hour of his departure is at hand, signalled symbolically by the arrival of Gentile "seekers after Jesus", prototypes or forerunners of the Gentile Church, precipitates in Christ a conflict of indecision. Deeply wrought up at the prospect of the death that awaits him, he cries, "What shall I say, 'Father, save me from this hour'? No, for this purpose I have come to this hour" (vs. 27). In this brief passage John presents the agony in Gethsemane. Though Jesus experiences human hesitance in the face of death, it is only momentary, and he quickly dispels it. The reassurance that comes over him brings renewed conviction that his whole mission culminating now in death is for the sake of others.

Specifically, the outcome of this last full measure of devotion will mean (1) the *krisis* or judgment of the world which chooses to remain in darkness by putting Jesus to death (vs. 31a); (2) a decisive turning of the tables on the sway of the Evil One in the world (vs. 31b); (3) the drawing together of the "sons of light" to his side (vs. 32). These themes on the meaning of the Passion will be further elaborated in the disciple-teaching that follows in chapters 13 through 17.

To the man of the world the event of Calvary takes its place with other historical events, no better and no worse than many another exhibition of man's inhumanity to man. But to the man who has experienced the unmasking of evil and its dethronement from the control of his life by the strength of Christ, Calvary is the truly decisive moment of his whole life. He knows what Paul means by dying with Christ that he may live with him (Rom. 6:8).

The Sum of the Matter (12:37-50)

The public ministry of Jesus has come to a close (vs. 36). The evangelist appends a reflection on the problem of the divided response to Christ (vss. 37-43). Then, in words attributed to the Lord, he draws up a summary of the meaning of this controversial ministry in the whole divine purpose of the Redeemer God (vss. 44-50).

The disbelief of Israel is set forth in terms similar to those used by Paul which describe the inscrutable purpose of God who appears to have blinded the eyes and hardened the hearts of disbelieving Jews, as Isaiah foretold (vss. 37-43; cf. Rom. 9). John is often charged with a strongly predestinarian point of view.[22] Two things need to be kept in mind: (1) John and other New Testament writers use a common Hebrew idiom in which a result is frequently viewed as the cause of an action; (2) there are many evidences that he assumed human choice and responsibility for actions. John divides men into two classes, it is true; those who have faith and those who do not; those who come to the light and those who remain in darkness. But the drawing by the Father of men unto himself occurs simultaneously with the free coming of the believer. "All that the Father gives me will come to me" (6:37a, cf. 44-45, 65). Throughout the New Testament this double emphasis appears: God's unchanging purpose and man's obligation to decide. Coming into life with God is always both an act of God's grace and man's responsible choice.

Verses 44-50 summarize the chief themes of the discussions and debates with the friends and foes met by Jesus in his ministry. Once again we hear of his mission in the world as a commission assigned by God (vss. 44-45). He has come as light into the awful darkness that engulfs a world turned aside from the divine purpose in creation (vs. 46). His mission is born out of a love for the life of men and no desire for their condemnation (vs. 47).

But the truth of who Jesus is and of what he says, the validity of his claim to be the Son of God and of his message, now frequently a matter of dispute and uncertainty, will be fully vindicated in God's own time. The love of God in Christ, if accepted, means life now and forever; conversely the rejection of that love brings condemnation. Like the Law for the Jew, Christ's words are the entry into life or the banishment to death (vs. 48).

In perfect keeping with the view of Christ taken throughout this Gospel, this section is brought to a close with a restatement of Christ's divine authority (or the derivative authority of Christ's words) and of his loving obedience to the Father (vss. 49-50). It is the glory of God he manifests; his praise he tells; his word of life he brings; his service he seeks —for himself and for all God's creatures—that God may "be all in all" (I Cor. 15:28, K.J.V.).

Throughout the language of spoken word, summarized in the Seven Similitudes, and in the enacted word, summarized in the Seven Signs, Christ has been presented to the reader as the New Torah, the true Messiah, the Son of God. But it will be the final events of his death and exaltation, the return that completes the coming, which once and for all will bestow the quickening Spirit and make possible a true understanding of what has really happened (cf. 7:39). John has brought us up to that decisive moment in his reading of that history and in his interpretations of its meaning for our time and life.

Chapter FIVE

Dying to Live

THE DISCOURSES IN THE UPPER ROOM are a unique feature of the Gospel of John. Among the best known and best loved sections of this interpretative Gospel study, chapters 13 through 17 present extensive teaching of the Lord in the intimacy of a meal with his disciples. One has only to recall such words as "A new commandment I give to you, that you love one another" or "Let not your hearts be troubled; believe in God, believe also in me" or "Greater love has no man than this, that a man lay down his life for his friends"—to realize that we are listening to words which have nourished Christian life through the centuries. Not without reason has this section been called the New Testament psalter.

What does the evangelist have in mind by inserting this teaching at this point in the narrative? The public ministry of Jesus has come to an end. Shortly, the story of those last tragic hours of Jesus' life will begin. Between the two, in the context of a final meal shared with his friends, we hear Jesus expound the meaning of his departure to the Father, his return to his disciples, the coming of the other Paraclete who is the Spirit of truth, and the new relationship of his present and prospective disciples through him to the Father. All of this, just before the retelling of the gripping events of the last hours.

The reason becomes clear. John believes that these words of the Lord contain the true explanation of all these final events. Here is unlocked the mystery of what is involved in the Crucifixion, the Resurrection and the Ascension of Jesus. Those events can never be understood simply as external verifiable occurrences. They must be viewed from within, seen from the perspective of his whole mission, if their full meaning is to be grasped and their power released. Here, then, is what John believed Jesus understood by *dying to live*. We might regard these instructions as the counterpart of the teaching about the suffering Son of man in the other Gospels. If so, the note of confidence and victory is sounded more clearly in John than elsewhere.

A Parabolic Act of Humble Service (13:1-30)

With the hour of his departure at hand, Jesus shares a simple supper meal with his disciples just before the beginning of the feast of the Passover and Unleavened Bread. If this is the supper described by the other evangelists, then John has set it at a different time. For Mark and the others the Last Supper is understood as a Passover meal, the traditional Seder of unleavened bread, bitter herbs, and roast lamb, eaten after sundown in the first hours of the 15th of the Jewish month, Nisan. John, however, dates the rendezvous in Jerusalem on the day before, on the 14th of Nisan; for he believes Jesus was crucified on the same afternoon that the Passover lambs were being slain in preparation for the evening repast. To him as to Paul, Christ is the true Paschal sacrifice (I Cor. 5:7).

We have already seen that John associates with the lakeside meal in Galilee much of the teaching which the other Gospel writers relate to this last supper with the disciples (see John 6:25-71). He makes no mention now of the familiar words spoken over the broken bread and the cup. Knowledge of that is common enough in the Church to be taken for granted. Instead he describes an incident occurring at the gathering which he believes explains the inner meaning of that meal, indeed, symbolized the whole life and servant ministry of him who was the *host!*

While they were eating, Jesus left his place and began to wash the feet of the men assembled around the table. It was a typical act of Oriental courtesy, an act which a host would order his servants to perform for dinner guests arriving with dust of the city's streets on their feet. Disciples might have performed such an act of service for their esteemed teachers, but it was an unheard of thing for a rabbi to demean himself in such a way before his students. Small wonder, then, that Peter's objection is voiced so violently: "You shall never wash my feet" (vs. 8).

The reply of Jesus is enigmatic, to put it mildly. The matter is further complicated by some obscurity in the form of the text. The longer form, probably the original, reads: "He who has bathed does not need to wash, except for his feet, but he is clean all over; and you are clean, but not all of you" (vs. 10). What was Peter supposed to understand from that? The question may be unanswerable, but we may be able to discern what the evangelist understood by it.

Religious washings were commonplace in the time of Jesus. There is evidence of numerous baptizing sects in Palestine in the first century of which the Essene community at Qumran offers one example. Apart from the baptismal ceremony for receiving Gentile converts into the membership of the Jewish community, these lustrations were always repeated regularly as a means of cleansing from ritual defilements. John seems to understand this saying of the Lord's, in part, as an allusion to the practice of Christian baptism. This is no rite continuously repeated. It is a once-for-all act by means of which one is fully forgiven for his past sin and set upon a new way.

But this purification and renewal is effective because of the servant ministry of the Lord brought to a climax in his sacrificial death. John's Gospel recognizes that Christian baptism is a baptism into the death and resurrection of Christ, just as Paul taught in Romans 6:3-4. Indeed, the Synoptic Gospels preserve two sayings of Jesus in which he himself interpreted his approaching death as a baptism to be undergone (see Mark 10:39; Luke 12:50).

The meaning of the phrase "except for his feet" in verse 10 is not at all clear. Some have suggested that this is a cryptic reference to the Lord's Supper, the second sacramental rite in the Church. Others prefer to regard it as a reference to a social custom which the evangelist has inserted. St. Augustine offers a suggestive interpretation, reminding us that despite our baptismal regeneration there is need for a daily repentance and purification as we walk through the dirt and dust of the world.

> Thus, he who intercedes for us washes our feet daily. That we are in need of washing our feet daily (which means that we ought to find the right path for our spiritual footsteps), this we confess in the Lord's prayer when we say, "Forgive us our debts, as we also forgive our debtors."[1]

It is just this reversal of roles as the world defines them which constitutes the nature of life in God's order. There the last of the world are the first, the servant is the master, the small are the great. The parabolic act of humility and service gives expression to a saying which Luke associates with the Last Supper. "For which is greater, one who sits at table, or one who serves? Is it not the one who sits at table? But I am among you as one who serves" (Luke 22:27).[2] The towel, as well as the bread and the wine, is a sacred symbol of the Lord who gives himself in selfless service for the life of the world.

The act completed, Jesus returns to his place and talks to his companions about what he has done (vss. 12-20). Far from being something unique and unrepeatable, the example he has set in this gesture of loving service is to be a model for their own ministry. "You also should do as I have done to you." Here is the real criterion by which Golden Rule conduct ought to be judged. Not simply doing as done by, but rather doing as *he* has done. A rather cheap level of action could pass muster if we were only required to do to others what we would like them to do to us. What Christ asks of his followers is that they reproduce in their relationships with others *what he has already done for them*. The difference between what we expect and what he expects may be considerable.

Christ's washing of the disciples' feet is not merely a symbol, an example he set of the Christian's service to others; it is also a sign that he is present in any act of service which meets the needs of men.

"Truly, truly, I say to you, he who receives any one whom I send receives me; and he who receives me receives him who sent me" (John 13:20; cf. Matt. 10:40 and parallels). The chain of command originates with the Sending Father, enters the world through the One whom he has sent, and finds extension in those whom he sends. Rightly to understand its mission in the world, the Church must know itself as the visible presence of God through Jesus Christ accomplishing his work in the world. Nothing less. The world truly meets God in the person of Christ as it should meet God in the company of Christ's companions.

Still defections occur; betrayed love is a tragic possibility. Even that first little company was not immune to it. With sorrow expressive of the same troubled heart, evident at the death of Lazarus (11:33, 38), Jesus confides his anxiety to his disciples (vss. 21-30). To the disciple immediately beside him at the board, he confides his fear that Judas, the treasurer of the little band, will betray him to the authorities. This man who reclined at his right when this confidential word was spoken is described simply as "the one whom Jesus loved." Though he remains unnamed in subsequent references in the Gospel,[3] the tradition is probably correct which identifies the beloved disciple with John bar Zebedee.

In the darkness of the evening, Judas, the child of darkness, made his abrupt exit. He too had shared that fellowship of love and received food from the Master's hands, but this was no proof of loyalty nor salvation. The significance of the sacramental act (the Lord's Supper) must be found in the underlying attitude of the participant and the consequences in action, John seems to say.

Before turning to the first of the valedictory addresses that follow, let us summarize the significance of this meal as John describes it. (1) First of all, in a primary way, the washing of the disciples' feet seems to interpret the meaning of the death of Christ for the believers. This act of humble love is a symbol of the Crucifixion, a mark of a life generously poured out for others in an atoning sacrifice. (2) This act brings a demand as well as a gift, however, for the life and death which it epitomizes set an example of service which they are obliged to make the model of their own way of life. (3) The act speaks to Christian worship, also, interpreting the inner meaning of Baptism and the Lord's Supper. Far from being liturgical rites alone, complete in themselves, these rites must manifest and lead into a fellowship of love marked by humility and loving service to human need.

DISCOURSE

(I). Love, Death and Hope, the Holy Spirit, the Church (13:31-14:31)

The valedictory addresses may be said to commence at 13:31. Though John assigns these words directly to the Upper Room setting, it is soon apparent that he is thinking in a larger way of the situation facing the Church in his own time. In a special way these chapters are to be seen as the reflections of the evangelist on sayings of Jesus, cast in the evangelist's own literary style and pointed toward problems of faith and church order in his own day.

Christ, for John and the early church, was not simply the Jesus of Galilee who once spoke to them; he was the reigning Christ who, in their own time, was now speaking to his own, still addressing them as their Lord. It has been suggested by some scholars that these addresses are developments of Christian sermons preached by the evangelist in his own church when the Lord's Supper was celebrated. This might well be, for the early church believed that it was Christ's own voice which spoke through the living word of Christian preachers. This belief ought always to be the glory and the anguish of the Christian pulpit. "Faith comes from what is heard, and what is heard comes by the preaching of Christ," is Paul's explanation of the whole enterprise of Christian preaching (Rom. 10:17).

Separation and Reunion. With the abrupt departure of Judas, Jesus turns to tell his disciples that the hour has come when through his death he is to be glorified (13:31-33). Glory in this Gospel is inseparable from Crucifixion (see 12:16, 23; 17:1). Truly understood, that death spells no final tragedy but the triumphant return of Jesus to his Father. By it he exchanges earthly rejection for heavenly glory. By that death, the Father who sent him on his mission is glorified.

The style in which John expresses Jesus' familiar saying about neighbor love adds a new dimension of meaning to the words found in the Synoptic Gospels (13:34-35). In Mark 12:31 and parallels, the "royal law" for the Christian[4] is quoted directly from the Law of Moses and reads, "You shall love your neighbor as yourself" (Lev. 19:18). Rabbi Akiba (died *ca.* A.D. 135) once observed of the precept, "This is a great, inclusive, fundamental truth in the Torah."

But what is to be the character of loving another "as yourself"? Everything depends on the quality of that self-love. It may be a neurotic infatuation with one's own securities and rights, whereas Jesus is obviously talking about a glowing desire and a resolute seeking after the best interests of the loved one. Perhaps it was his concern to make clear what the standard of true love really is that led John to reformulate the Torah precept. "Love one another; *even as I have loved you* . . . you also love one another" (13:34; cf. 15:12). The kind of love for us God has dramatized in Christ sets the standard for the quality of love we are to manifest in our dealings with others! "The tests of membership in Christ's Church," wrote C. J. Wright, "have included belief in dogmatic statement and obedience to the laws of the institution but have not always included *love* to *one another*." [5]

In John 14 attention is turned to the problem of death and separation. The little company which had been through so much together is now threatened by the loss of its leader and the disruption of the fellowship. How is it to survive, bereft of the beloved teacher? Jesus reassures them:

> Set your troubled hearts at rest. Trust in God always; trust also in me. There are many dwelling-places [or rooms] in my Father's house; if it were not so I should have told you; for I am going there on purpose to prepare a place for you.
> — *John* 14:1-2, N.E.B.[6]

In John's Gospel the return of Christ to his own is interpreted in several ways. Here is one of them. He promises to come again at the moment of the believer's death to receive him into the heavenly mansion and bring him to the presence of the Father-God. "Heaven is my home!" That has been a Christian cry of hope through the ages. Yes, but the gospel promise of eternal life with God should not be interpreted as the assurance of an endless rocking-chair existence, or pleasures of a worldly sort, but *living with God!*

How do we know this? How are we to be sure of it? The confidence that he who promises it is the true revealer of the Father is John's answer. Three vivid metaphors express the nature and purpose of Christ among men. "I am the way [a road to the Father];[7] I am the truth [a revelation of reality in contrast to appearances];[8] I am the life [what it means to be alive to God]"[9] (14:6).

Now it is the disciple Philip who voices the petulant request of the unbelieving and the half-believing world. "Give us a sign." Seeing is believing. He cannot understand that there is no single incontrovertible fact that can force belief. Faith is a matter of daring commitment, of costly decision, of running risks. It calls for a spiritual perception beyond ordinary sight and rules of evidence. Either Philip has seen the Father in the whole life of Jesus—in the whole conduct of the mission—or he has seen only a man aspiring to grandiose honors (10:33; 19:5). It is the true God who is made known in what Jesus says and does. Jesus' ministry of service must carry its own voiceless testimony that he is not an idealist, philanthropist, nor humanitarian, but the *revealer* of the Father. This work that he is doing is not his own but God's work in the world.

The end has not yet been seen. Christ's own departure to heavenly glory will open up a new and enlarged scope for his mission among men. This promise of greater works yet to be done (14:12) is probably to be understood as a prediction of the whole Gentile mission of the Church, winning converts to the faith from all the nations. But the missioners are not left to their own desires and devices. These greater deeds are to be accomplished by the power of Christ the worker in them. The mission will be blessed by his support when it is carried on "in his name," consistent with the ideals and aims that have marked their life together during his earthly ministry (vss. 13-14).[10]

There is surely no assurance here that any prayer request will be honored as long as it is stamped by a proper credential, "in thy name." Those prayers are fulfilled which are in harmony with the divine will. Jesus' whole message and activity centers in that holy purpose: the coming of God's kingdom. This must be the center and soul of all truly Christian petition.

The Ministry of the Holy Spirit. At this point we are introduced to a new name: the Paraclete, to give an English spelling to the Greek word. There are five passages in the Gospel where the Paraclete is mentioned; this is the first (14:16-17).[11] Other titles are used, also. He is called the Spirit of truth, a name found in the Dead Sea Scrolls, also,[12] as well as the Holy Spirit.

In secular Greek of the day the word *paraklētos* had a juridical connotation, signifying a legal assistant, advocate or patron. In biblical usage it is related to words describing prophetic exhortation[13] and the messianic salvation.[14] With so rich an association of meaning the word defies any single sufficient translation. Comforter (K.J.V.), Counselor (R.S.V.), Helper(Moffatt), Advocate (N.E.B.) have all been used.

We shall not be bound by any single English equivalent, but it is of vital importance to recognize what underlies the word-symbols we use. The whole span of Jesus' career including his earthly ministry and his post-resurrection reign are comprehended in the term. His ministry in the flesh as the Jesus of history may be so described (vs. 16), as can his work continued as the victorious Lord, the Christ of Easter faith (vss. 18, 26; I John 2:1). *The Spirit of Christ continues to speak in the word of Christian preaching which declares the good news of God's salvation.* This was just the character of Jesus' ministry before Easter and this continues to be his function through the Church after Easter. His followers are not to be left friendless and leaderless. "I will come to you" (John 14:18).

The coming of the Spirit, who is none other than the Spirit of Christ himself, takes place following the departure of the earthly Jesus from the world.

Here we are presented with a second aspect of Christ's coming to the world. The second Advent has already been described as his coming at the death of the individual disciple to take him home (vs. 3). In the present passage Christ pledges to manifest himself in the present Christian experience of the faithful disciple and the Church (vs. 23). The Church is the community of those who celebrate the continuing presence of the risen Lord with his people and share his work in the world. The joy of unbroken fellowship with him and the Father is the experience of those who truly love him and keep his commandments.

There is no true love without obedience; the one is the obverse of the other (14:15, 21, 23-24; 15:10). So this promise of Christ's coming is fulfilled wherever the Church is redemptively involved in society doing the work of Christ, dealing with the sick and the sad, attacking both the visible effects and hidden causes of poverty, concerned about the dispossessed, applying reconciling love in conflict situations, willing to be completely and utterly spent in the service of God's cause in the world (vss. 22-24; Acts 10:41).

In a second Paraclete saying we learn that it is his function not to supersede but to continue the very same ministry in the world which Jesus began (John 14:26). From that day to this all sorts of bizarre views and outlandish actions have been countenanced at times as a special inspiration of the Spirit moving upon believers. From the Montanists of the second century to extreme Pentecostalists of the twentieth, men have believed themselves to be the recipients of special revelations from the Spirit. It may be. But the Gospel of John presents a single criterion for judging Spirit guidances which is often overlooked. *What is claimed as inspiration must be consistent with the mind and action of the historical Jesus known to us in the Scriptures.* The Helper is a teacher who will "bring to your remembrance all that I have said to you" (vs. 26). John will make that point several times.

Jesus' word of farewell is in the form of the familiar Jewish blessing *shalom* [peace] (vs. 27; cf. 16:33). But the peace he gives is no half-conscious greeting or perfunctory word. His peace rises out of a world of reality beyond, enters into our midst, and blesses those who live and serve here, driving out fear with the confidence that Christ is with them as he promised.[15] Thus there is no cause to fear even the powers of evil in the world. They are no match against God's Son who conquers them through the cross.[16] Luther's immortal hymn paraphrases the thought of verse 30 as the testimony of the Church.

> The Prince of Darkness grim,
> We tremble not for him;
> His rage we can endure,
> For lo, his doom is sure,
> One little word shall fell him.

DISCOURSE

(II). Death, Hope, the Holy Spirit, the Church (15:1-16:33)

The same principal themes that were present in the previous chapter now reappear in chapters 15 and 16, only in fuller, more colorful statement.[17] It is as though the initial statement of a musical line played in direct fashion is now subject to an elaboration in varied symphonic patterns of point and counterpoint.

The True Vine (15:1-17). The parable of the true Vine introduces Part II of the address. In what may have been intended by John to be another interpretation of the Lord's Supper (cf. chap. 6), as well as a larger reference to the nature of the Church, we are presented with a metaphor of unity in the form of a viticultural figure. It is thoroughly familiar to readers of the Old Testament. The vine often appears as a symbol of faithful Israel tended by the master vinedresser, God.[18] To speak of Christ as the true Vine, therefore, is equivalent to saying that he alone within the nation represents the true and faithful people of God.[19]

Two emphases are made in the parable: the necessity for fruitfulness and unity. Pruning is essential to a healthy vine; the dead wood must be cut away to increase its productivity. Even fruiting wood is subject to the discipline of pruning that it may bear more bountifully. Applied to the Church the figure suggests both apostate Christians who have defaulted on their vows and also lethargic members whose enthusiasm has dimmed and faded and whose devotion has cooled and relaxed. As Jesus had insisted (in the Synoptic Gospels[20]), the evidence of discipleship is not displayed in pat recitations of "Lord, Lord" nor in dutiful liturgical practices, but in concrete acts of love toward others (vs. 8).

Such mutual love which unites the Father and the Son is that which binds the true disciples together to them (vss. 9-10, 13; cf. 14:21, 23). Such love is not to be confused with some natural sentiment nor cheapened to a romantic attachment. The realization that the love practiced by Christians must be like the love which marks the relationship uniting the Father with the Son (which exists between the Father and the Son) is disturbing! It exposes many of our claims of brotherly affection as poor efforts at the very best, fraudulent imitations at the worst.

Yet Jesus' word is spoken, he says, not to drive us to complete self-despair, but "that my [his] joy may be in you" (vs. 11). God's frozen people, as the Church has recently been called, could be thawed out by the warmth of Christian joy radiating through them! Sour-faced, joyless, pulse-taking Christianity has little in common with the true *enthusiasm* (the word means God-intoxication) of the believer. Some Christians, it has been rightly observed, have just enough religion to make them miserable. Where the joy of Christ is known and shared, the Church is no longer a self-defensive, complaining company, weary of the march, but a self-forgetting, singing, pilgrim people en route to a heavenly goal.

We have already heard the new commandment which Christ lays upon his followers (13:34-35). Now it is mentioned again and elaborated (15:12-17). The true lover always believes himself expendable. He willingly surrenders all, even his very life if necessary, for the sake of his beloved. In Romans 5:6-11 Paul provides us with a commentary on what it means to say that Christ lays down his life for his friends.

The present passage in John shows the struggle of new thought with the obtuseness of customary language. To speak of men as subjects and servants of God is accurate enough if God is to be thought of only as King and Judge. But what shall be said of the relationship when the Almighty is known as Father? Daring and dangerous as the name "friends" may be when improperly used, it can be given to those devoted in love and obedience to the Son and the Father. Without forfeiting the essential understanding of obedience, the vocabulary of servitude yields to the language of sonship and friendship to denote the God-man relationship.[21] "Friendship . . . is the final word in the dialogue between God and man, because God's ultimate word to mankind is *Christ*." [22]

We cannot overlook verse 16 (cf. vs. 19) and its implications for a true understanding of the Church. What is the basis for membership in the Church? If Christ chooses us, as this saying unequivocally declares, how can we presume by human qualifications to determine who can or cannot be admitted to fellowship with us? Our churches need to take to heart and practice the words that came from the New Delhi Assembly of the World Council of Churches, "Our brethren in Christ are given to us, not chosen by us."[23]

Facing Hostility (15:18-27). In all the Gospels Jesus is represented as reminding candidates to discipleship that his way runs counter to the way of the world. Misunderstanding, ridicule, outright acts of violence are sure to be aroused. This is no primrose path to glory; it is a hazardous way, a *via dolorosa* (vss. 18-25). The faithful disciple can no more avoid getting into trouble with society than he can deny his Lord! It cannot be otherwise until society itself has been claimed for the kingdom of God. But of two things the disciple must be sure: (1) He must meet cursing with blessing, not self-pity or retaliatory violence—either by thought, word, or act; (2) He must give no offense to others except for the sake of the gospel, not for any other reason.

The way in which we meet the hatred of the world shows the measure of our devotion to Christ and of our acceptance of his way. It is possible, though, for the Church to be rightly criticised for the wrong reason. To face public criticism because the Church demands unreasonable privileges in tax exemptions or because it seeks to maintain itself as an exclusivist—segregated—club is scarcely to be hated for the sake of Christ and the gospel!

The chapter closes with the third reference to the coming of the Counselor (vss. 26-27). Again it is emphasized that the function of the Spirit of truth is not to bring some new and independent revelation, such as the new scriptures of early heretics like Montanus or the golden books of Joseph Smith. Every claim to inspiration by the Spirit must be tested against the truth as it has been revealed to us in Jesus Christ. The Spirit's role in the life of the Church is to bear witness to the whole historical work of Jesus. This, too, is the function of the disciples who have been with him from the outset of the program. The Church, to be the Church, must always be engaged in witness.

So crucially important are the insights into the true nature of the Church in this single chapter alone that we may pause for a moment to add them up. The Church, we hear, is a community of Christ's folk who are completely involved with and dependent upon him (vss. 4-7); they are expected to be productive, not parasitic (vs. 8); they are treated by their Lord as friends rather than as menials (vss. 13-15); they are chosen rather than self-appointed (vs. 16); they are prepared to pay the cost of discipleship (vss. 18-21); they are ambassadors of the truth to all the world (vs. 27). That is quite an order. But it is what Christ means his Church to be!

The Spirit as Judge (16:1-11). The work of the Counselor is further defined in chapter 16. After another solemn warning that the opposition to Jesus and to his followers results from the failure to grasp the will of God and to recognize his purposes, Jesus comments on the discomfiture of his disciples. In truth they are more preoccupied about themselves and their grief than they are about the future of God's work in the world. Their sorrow is occasioned more by personal fears about their own welfare than by what will happen to him. Instead they should be trying to understand how this separation will mark a transition to a new and larger phase of God's program, as he has been insisting all along (vss. 1-6).

The coming of the Counselor is conditional upon the completion of the present part of that program (vs. 7). The death and exaltation of Christ will become the means whereby the Spirit of Jesus will be let loose in all the world to continue the work begun here in Palestine. Three specific actions of the Helper-Spirit are set out in verse 8. Each of them is couched in language which is somewhat obscure, so we need to look at them carefully.

In the first place, it is said that the Spirit will "convince the world of sin." The verb means to bring to conviction or to expose. Following the clue given in the succeeding verse, we may say that one function of the Spirit is to expose the real basis of mankind's sin, namely the rejection of the Revealer. Men have seen the things he has done; yet the reaction in general has been indifference or antagonism, not acceptance. The light from heaven has shone; yet men have edged back furtively into the darkness. They cannot bring themselves to decide for (accept) God even though he has decided for them; that is why they stand convicted of sin.[24]

Sin is not reducible here to matters of moralism. Throughout the Bible there is a distinction between sins (plural) and sin (singular). In itself sin does not consist of a particular act but of a total condition of life. It means the disavowal of God as the ruling center of one's life, a set of the will in defiance of his will, an act of treason against his Kingdom. Individual sins are symptomatic expressions of this basic condition, but the condition cannot be corrected by treating the symptoms apart from their source. John is consistent with the whole biblical witness when he identifies the fundamental basis of sin as an attitude of disbelief and a rejection of God's overture of friendship.

Secondly, the Spirit will convict the world through the witness of the Church for failing to recognize Jesus' life, death, and exaltation as a manifestation of the righteousness of God in action. So, too, Paul had earlier declared that the real meaning of the cross was not a Roman-Jewish reprisal to subversive ambition but a declaration of the divine love and righteousness (Rom. 3:26 and 5:8). Finally, the Spirit will trouble the conscience of the world about its false judgment of the One sent from God. In their stubborn arrogance men think Jesus has been tried and convicted as an impostor and blasphemer. In point of fact it is they who have been judged, not he. The cross actually exposes the diabolical work of Satan and his human henchmen. They are shown up for what they are: God-haters and trouble makers.[25]

Outwardly, the world has won. Pilate remains in power; the Sanhedrin continues its work; the king-for-a-day has had his day. But the Spirit, coming as the Son's gift upon his return to the Father, will open the eyes of the disciples to the true state of affairs and send them off on the run to tell the good news. It is the Spirit's task to drive this home to every new generation of believers, just as it is their exciting responsibility to preach and practice it. This is how the Spirit carries on his work through the Church in the world.

The Spirit as Teacher (16:12-15). The last of the five Paraclete passages follows (vss. 12-15). In the clearest terms yet, the work of the Spirit as guide and teacher is described. "He will take what is mine and declare it to you" (vs. 14). The truth has already been given by God in Jesus' ministry, but it cannot be grasped completely or all at once. Through the guidance of the Spirit working in the Church in its preaching and teaching the full dimensions of that truth will be explored and brought to bear upon the lives of its members and upon the world beyond their fellowship. "The things that are to come" (vs. 13) are the final issues of judgment and salvation already active in the present through the work of the Spirit. John's Gospel gives us new and necessary insights into the relationships between Christ, the Spirit, the Church, preaching, and truth as discovery.

What Lies Ahead (16:16-24). The things Jesus has been saying cause all sorts of questions to arise. Dialogue resumes as the disciples speculate among themselves what can be meant by "a little while" [26] and all this talk about seeing and not seeing. They are confused and apprehensive.

Jesus' reply evidences a tender concern for them in their anxiety. But how is one to make clear what is in prospect and how it is to be understood? He promises that the interval of separation will be brief, but the language he uses gives no single indication of the time of his return. Perhaps it is left vague purposely. After all, John is convinced, as we have seen, that the return of the Lord cannot be identified solely with his coming at the end of the world, as so many apparently imagine. The "little while," then, refers not only to the rapid passing away of the present age as God's purpose comes to consummation. The return of Christ in the Easter appearances and his presence as the Spirit in the Church are, we believe, also promised here.

After these events have transpired, such questions as the disciples then nervously raised will not need to be asked (vs. 23). If that is so, then some of the questions we continue to raise today may indicate that we have not yet entered into the fullness of Easter experience and joy. It must be said immediately that there is nothing here that denies the right and need for questions. Only it is the *right* questions, of an increasingly mature sort, which ought to be raised, not those voiced over and over again that belong on the beginner's level (cf. Heb. 6:1-3).

On Speaking Too Fast and Too Soon (16:25-33). Here is a frank admission of the limitations of language to convey the whole truth of Jesus' message. The issues of life and death, Jesus declares, have been deliberately presented in figurative, symbolic speech (vs. 25; cf. 10:6). Even so, his teaching has remained obscure to the general public and has confused his own inner circle. Plain speech would be unpalatable for them at this stage of their maturing in faith. As if to prove the point, the origin and destination of Jesus' mission is now defined straightforwardly. "I came from the Father and have come into the world; again, I am leaving the world and going to the Father" (vs. 28). In a grand rush the disciples assure him that now they understand him fully and believe him. But it becomes clear in the light of succeeding events that this is not the case. These men are soon to find themselves disillusioned and dispersed, each returning to his own home.

All they can do now is to listen and later remember his promise, "Be of good cheer, I have overcome the world." Only after his return to the Father will they be convinced that the world may struggle against God, but it can never defeat him.

The cross will appear to advertise to everyone, "God is dead." But Easter faith with its enlightenment by the Spirit who leads men to the truth will give the real answer. "I have overcome the world" (vs. 33).

The Prayer of the Lord (17:1-26)

Several prayers of Jesus are recorded in this Gospel. There is the prayer uttered before the tomb of Lazarus (11:41f.) and the prayer wrung out of an agony of spirit at the prospect of suffering and death (12:27). The present prayer, which brings the valedictory addresses to a close, is the longest of all those found in the Gospels.

Actually it is a combination of elements, including both direct words of the Savior, as John believes, together with the writer's own reflections upon them (see for example vs. 3). In its present form it gathers up the chief emphases of the message and work of Jesus, just as Part I of the Gospel concluded with a summary statement (12:44-50). Cast in liturgical form, the words take on a rich splendor. The Lord in prayer brings before the Father his own work (now about to be completed); the band of disciples who will continue that work; and the future Church that will result from their missionary efforts.

The first movement of the prayer is concerned with Jesus' own ministry (vss. 1-8). The long-anticipated climactic hour is now striking. It is the hour of his death at the hands of angry men, but it will prove to be the hour of his glorification as he returns to the One who sent him on this mission of salvation into the world. He has glorified the Father in a ministry faithful unto death and the Father will glorify him and vindicate him from the false judgments of the men who put him to death. God is glorified in that men are already beginning to experience the new life which is his gift.

We are to identify in verse 3 a valuable insight into the meaning of "life eternal" in this Gospel. What does it mean to have eternal life? It means that we *know* the only true God; that is, we enter into a personal relationship with the Father and the Son.[27] In the Fourth Gospel knowing God is equivalent to believing (6:69; 17:8, 23), obeying (12:50; 14:23), abiding in—living in—(14:23; 15:4-10). To know God is something more than having an ability to discuss theological questions in a learned way—or even to participate in all the forms of the religious life including Bible study. *Knowing God* involves that intimacy of thought, sharing of the self, and commitment to common purposes, which mark the relationship between lovers. Where these exist, with the divine, there is a new quality of life — fittingly called *immortal*.

With that, the thought turns toward the disciples and what is in store for them (vss. 9-19). Chosen out of the world, their responsibility is to remain *within* it and to serve (vss. 11, 15). This vocation of the Christian is being discovered today in a new way. Reports one parishioner: "[Our pastor has] showed us that the church is only a place where we go for an hour to rehearse for a meeting with God in the world the other 167 hours a week."[28]

The disciples have been set apart, dedicated to the same mission as that to which Christ himself is dedicated. It is significant that here (as well as in 10:36) consecration is spoken of in the context of mission. As Christ is the One Sent, so they are also a people who are sent (vs. 18). When we speak of the Church as a gathered fellowship we must never forget that this is an incomplete description. The gathering takes place in order that the sending may be made possible. It is a sad mistake to locate the Church only in the houses of worship in which Christians assemble, though it surely ought to be there. The Church is found also in the business office, kitchen, shop, and schoolroom, wherever Christ's people are present and faithfully engaged upon their work. In this sense, it is neither a *place* nor a *social organization*, but an *event*, something that happens when Christ breaks into the lives of persons.

In the final movement of the prayer, Christ's concern widens to embrace not only the present small company of his followers but the whole number of those who will be brought to faith and life as the mission continues into the world (vss. 20-26). It is striking to note the way unity and mission are brought together throughout this section. Christ has already prayed for harmony among the disciples, a harmony-unity like that which exists between the

Father and the Son (vs. 11). Now a new thought is added. The effectiveness of the evangelical mission to the world is conditional upon the realization of brotherly unity within the fellowship of believers! "That they may all be one . . . *so that* the world may believe that thou hast sent me" (vs. 21; cf. 23).

A series of interlocking relationships characterize this unity. As the Father is in the Son and the Son in the Father, so believers are to be united together in them. If the need of such complete unity is to be taken as seriously as John intended (the church in his time may have been threatened by factionalism), then the reverse is also true. Any lack of unity or evidence of rivalry is a hindrance to the effectiveness of the Church's mission to the world.

This much is clear: the call to unity among the people of God cannot be made to depend upon a desire for more efficient church management or a concern for numerical strength to enforce its message. It must be heard as the call of Christ to his people for the sake of the mission of salvation to a needy world. The basis for the unity of the Church, and eventually, the unity of mankind is to be found in the very nature of God and his will. As God is one, so men are to be one. As God wills unity with him, so the Church must declare it and demonstrate it.[29] It is the New Jerusalem, not the Tower of Babel, which is the model of humanity, a model finding preliminary realization in the Church. We are forced to conclude from this that where that brotherhood and unity in God are lacking, then the church has lost its identity as the Church.

Here, then, is the prayer the Lord prays. How do we pray? W. H. Auden's answer to that stands in sorry contrast to what we have been hearing. Listen to what he considers to be an all too typical prayer.

> O God, put away justice and truth for we cannot understand them and do not want them. Eternity would bore us dreadfully. Leave thy heavens and come down to our earth of waterclocks and hedges. Become our uncle. Look after Baby, amuse Grandfather, escort Madam to the Opera, help Willy with his home-work, introduce Muriel to a handsome naval officer. Be interesting and weak like us, and we will love you as we love ourselves.[30]

A devastating caricature, but how inaccurate it is, is open to discussion.

The words are finished. Action resumes. In the last, swift, terrible hours, Roman justice with Jewish collusion will make its bid to bring Jesus to the silence of oblivion. But it will prove to be a short-lived triumph.

Chapter SIX

The Lord of Life
and Death

WHILE THERE IS SUBSTANTIAL AGREEMENT among the four Gospels about Jesus' arrest and trial, there are many puzzling differences in detail. If we compare the description of the proceedings with what is known of the juridical role of the Great Sanhedrin, a number of contradictions appear. Perhaps we are to understand that the trial of Jesus of Nazareth did not follow an official form at all, but rather was a hasty hearing before Jewish authorities who then handed him over to the Roman governor for execution. With a number of modern scholars we may conclude that the Jewish High Court had already decided, perhaps in collusion with the governor, to swear out a warrant against the Galilean teacher as a ringleader in subversive activities. He was then to be bound over to the Romans as a public warning against all agitators and seditionists. The death sentence, by agreement, was to be delivered by the Roman tribunal to avoid the risk of a public uprising by his friends and sympathizers.

The Arrest and Hearing Before Caiaphas (18:1-27)

Beyond the watercourse, Kidron, on the east side of the city of Jerusalem, rise the slopes of the Mount of Olives. On the lower side of the western face an olive orchard with an oil press, called in Hebrew *Gat Shemanim*, (Gethsemane) was a favorite place of retreat for Jesus and his disciples from the noisy crowded city (vs. 2). It was here that Jesus was seized under cover of darkness by a detachment of soldiers led by one of his own disciples.

John, alone of the evangelists, involves the Romans this early in the story, stating that the Temple police were accompanied by a cohort of Roman soldiers (vss. 3, 12).[1] It is John, too, who preserves an old tradition which assigns to an earlier date a Council decision to put an end to Jesus and the popular movement he was leading. "If we let him go on thus, everyone will believe in him, and the Romans will come and destroy both our holy place and our nation," they argued (11:48). Displaying characteristically independent action, Jesus gives himself up to the authorities with an emphatic, "I am he." In Jesus' plea for the safety of his associates, John believes that a word from the prayer in the upper room finds fulfillment (vss. 8, 9; cf. 17:12).

The Synoptic detail about the show of resistance among the disciples (Mark 14:47 and parallels) is elaborated by John; both the knife-wielder and the victim are identified by name. But in place of Luke's mention of the healing of the slave's ear, John adds Jesus' word about the necessity of submitting to the divine purpose of suffering and death. We do not hear Gethsemane's agonized cry in prayer:: "Abba, Father, . . . remove this cup from me" (Mark 14:36). Instead there is the steady assurance that countered that appeal, "Shall I not drink the cup which the Father has given me?" (John 18:11) This, not Peter's, is the true resistance to evil: *forbearance*, *forgiveness*, the *acceptance* of undeserved suffering, and a *confidence* in the eventual destruction of evil.

With that the prisoner is escorted to the home of the high priest Joseph called Caiaphas who lived in the southwest section of the city. John makes no explicit mention of any appearance of Jesus before the entire Council as the Synoptic writers do.[2] But it would have been in order for the president of the Court to examine a Jewish citizen before he was arraigned before the Roman magistrate. Even if the decision had already been made to get rid of this troublemaker, Pilate would probably require some specific indictment from the Jewish officials.

We may assume that the former high priest Annas who held office from A.D. 6 to 15 lived with his son-in-law Caiaphas, the incumbent high priest and president of the Court. It is not clear why Jesus was questioned by both men although this may be a reminiscence of the two appearances before the High Court listed by Mark (Mark 14:53; 15:1).

Who is the anonymous disciple who had access to the private quarters of the high priest and who accompanied Jesus inside while Peter hung back outside the door (John 18:15-16)? We do not know. But it is doubtful that he can be identified with any one of the twelve. As a result of his influence, Peter was admitted to the courtyard and fell in with a group of slaves and police who were warming themselves by a charcoal brazier. Without any trace of the emotion which pervades the tense scene of the denial by Peter in the Synoptics, John simply reports his words: "I am not [his disciple]" (vss. 17, 25, 27).

No question is put to Jesus by the high priest about his messianic ambitions and no such reply is made as we find in the other Gospels. When he is asked about his teaching and his following, Jesus parries the questions, suggesting that they ask those who have heard him preach (vs. 21). The gospel of eternal life, the evangelist wants us to understand, is no secret teaching designed for an elect few, but good news available to all who will give ear and obey. The result of what is considered to be an impertinent reply is a blow from one of the guards. It is another instance of the physical violence which our Gospel has noted as the common reaction to unanswerable argument.[3] Stone-throwing and name-calling are still the futile responses of little men to unwelcome truth.

The Kingdom of Christ and the Kingdom of Caesar (18:28-19:16)

Thus far we have not been told what specific charge has been lodged against Jesus by the Jews. That comes out in the official Roman trial. More than the other writers, John emphasizes the issue of kingship.[4] It is historically probable that the Roman court tried Jesus on a political charge of insurrection against the state. The question of messiahship as such, it is often pointed out, would have no interest for a Roman official. Only if messiahship was considered a royal office would it be recognized as a seditious claim against the supremacy of the emperor.

The praetorium, or official residence of the Roman emperor's agent in Jerusalem, was the former palace of Herod the Great, located in the northwest section of the city. The drama of the trial moves swiftly now but in more detail. How much is historically accurate, and how much is due to literary embellishment of the earlier record, it is difficult to say. But John strikingly represents the confrontation of two kingdoms here: the might and the majesty of Rome, symbol of earthly government, as brought to bear against the "kingship" which "is not of this world" (vs. 36) yet which has begun to exert its influence upon this world. John sees that in the truest sense it is Caesar, not Christ, who is on trial here.[5]

John agrees with the Synoptics in fixing upon the Jewish leaders the initiative for the arrest and the pressure for the death sentence. Pilate is represented as a fair-minded person, moved by sympathy toward this victim of an official plot, reluctant to endorse what he senses to be a miscarriage of justice. We must bear in mind that by the time the Gospels were being written the Christian movement was already pushing into the Roman world, often encountering suspicion and opposition—both in the form of social ostracism and physical violence. It would be understandable in the face of these pressures that the Gospel writers might play down the culpability of the Roman government in investigating and blocking the popular movement led by Jesus. Moreover, it must be doubted that Pilate acted only because the Jewish authorities could not execute the death sentence, as John believes (18:31). Modern historical research indicates that Jewish courts were not deprived of that prerogative at that time.[6]

Jesus' reply to the question, "Are you the King of the Jews?" is equivocal here, as it is in Matthew and Luke. He deflects the question returning it to the inquirer: What does Pilate think? Reference to the truth (*i.e.* the message of eternal life, vs. 37) to which Jesus bears testimony prompts a half-quizzical, half-pitying response from the governor, "What is truth?" (vs. 38) The conversation is abruptly closed; the practical-minded Roman isn't interested in such Eastern musings.

Contrary to Roman judicial procedure, Pilate orders the prisoner flogged, evidently as a substitute for the execution which he wants to avoid. The palace guard burlesques this ridiculous candidate

THE LORD OF LIFE AND DEATH 147

for royal honors by fashioning a makeshift crown and throwing over Jesus' shoulders a worn cloak to signify the imperial purple. But the accusers will not be put off. They would rather have a revolutionist like Jesus bar Abbas [Barabbas] given clemency than permit this Galilean to be freed![7] (18:39-40; 19:6) They sense intuitively who is the more dangerous.

So a second time the representatives of the two kingdoms confront each other (19:9ff.). A charge has now been clearly specified by the Jewish leaders. Jesus is guilty of blasphemy, they allege; "He has made himself the Son of God" (19:7). Blasphemy as a religious crime (cf. Lev. 24:16) would have been a matter of indifference to Pilate, but as an imperial officer he might have recognized in the accusation one of the many laudatory titles borne by the head of the state.[8] The accusers drove the point home. "If you release this man, you are not Caesar's friend; every one who makes himself a king sets himself against Caesar" (19:12). It might be replied that everyone who supports the cause of an absolute despot is no friend of God. But, then *and* since, men have been more nervously anxious to please Caesar than God!

In proper Roman custom Pilate takes his place on the rostrum or judgment seat.[9] The date and the hour are noted. It is high noon on Nisan 14, the day prior to the feast of the Passover (vs. 14).[10] "Here is your King!" Pilate announces. The words are intended as bitter irony. Just as the high priest earlier had all unwittingly spoken the real truth about Jesus (11:49f.), so the emperor's envoy in Palestine says more than he knows as he presents the prisoner before his enemies. The sentence is given. Jesus will be crucified as a traitor to the empire on the capital crime of diminishing the majesty of the state (*crimen laesae maiestatis*). But John believes that it is the Jewish officials who have committed the real blasphemy. In their protests, "We have no king but Caesar" (19:15), they have denied Israel's time-honored conviction that the God of Israel alone is their true king.

"It Is Finished" (19:17-42)

In his own characteristic way, John retells the story of the death and burial of the Lord. No one assists Jesus as the death march moves out from the praetorium to Hangman's Hill.[11] He carries the weight of the crossbeam unaided. Attached to the beam was a *titulus* [placard] advertising the nature of the condemned man's crime. John gives the most elaborate form of the inscription and specifies that it was trilingual. "Jesus of Nazareth, the King of the Jews" (vs. 19). When the Jews remonstrate that this is an utterly fraudulent claim, Pilate responds with a typical Latinism "What I have written, I have written" (*Quod scripsi, scripsi*). Once again we note the way in which our evangelist represents the opponents of Jesus as inadvertently declaring the real truth about him.

Even in the matter-of-fact distribution of Jesus' clothes among the four members of the execution squad John finds some special meaning. He tells us that the undergarment or tunic was a seamless piece of cloth (assuming that the discerning reader will recall that this type of garment was worn by the high priest [Lev. 16:4]).[12] Christ is the true high priest whose voluntary suffering and death is the perfect sacrifice atoning for the sins of the world.[13] The cross will become the means of bringing together into one great fellowship of love a presently scattered and divided humanity. The reality of the Church, the body of believers united in him, is made possible by this great redemptive event.

The spectacle of torturous death by crucifixion was not strange to the eyes of Palestinian commoners. Rome reserved this form of capital punishment for runaway slaves, insubordinate provincials, and common criminals. "Don't go on threatening," cries a slave in one of Plautus' plays. "Well I know the cross will be my end, my place of burial. There is where my ancestors all rest."[14] Edith Hamilton tells us that

> in Rome after the great slave insurrection the main road to the city was lined for more than a mile with the crosses of crucified slaves.[15]

But friends and relatives never cease to mourn for their men. So in this sad hour outside Jerusalem a group keeps vigil as the tragedy is enacted.

John's Gospel alone describes an incident in which

the dying Lord commits his mother to the care of the beloved disciple (vs. 26). Perhaps this reflects a later tradition that Mary and John the disciple lived in the city of Ephesus until their deaths. However, in the post-Easter scene of Acts 1:14 the mother of Jesus is with her sons rather than with John. Indeed we would expect that the brothers of Jesus would have accepted their filial responsibility to care for their mother after the death of her first-born son. John, however, is less concerned with the historical relationships as such than to see in this reminiscence a symbol of the new community of the Church brought into existence through the death and resurrection of the Lord.

The sour wine which was lifted to wet the lips of the dying man may have been *posca*, a favorite drink of Roman soldiers. With this, John reports, Jesus uttered his final words, "It is finished" (vs. 30). It is likely that John intends the reader to appreciate a deeper meaning in those words than that Jesus' life is at an end, though that is certainly included. In a larger sense the words mean: My work is completed; the task is fulfilled.

It was not uncommon for victims of crucifixion to linger for two or three days before death brought a release from their agonies. The soldiers who were ordered to hasten death for the three men at Golgotha were surprised to discover that one of them, the messianic pretender, had already expired.

We cannot be sure about the significance of the detail that John adds. Surely any suspicion that Jesus had not really died but had only lost consciousness would be dispelled by an eye witness' report that he had been pierced by a soldier's spear (vs. 34). That he merely lost consciousness and had not died was in fact a Jewish allegation intended to refute the apostolic preaching of the Resurrection. Even certain Gnostic Christians held the strange view that the true Son of God only *appeared* to suffer and die on the cross. John emphasizes that his death was *real*, not a pretense or deception. He would agree with the theology of the cross held by the author of the Letter to the Hebrews, "We see Jesus . . . crowned with glory and honor because of the suffering of death, so that by the grace of God he might taste death for every one" (Heb. 2:9).

What we have come to know about John leads us to look for theological meanings rather than historical details. In the reference to the blood and water that flowed from the wound, John probably saw a symbol of the relation between the life-giving sacraments and the death of Christ. Christ is the source and the sustenance of that new life from above figured in the birth by water and the Spirit in the conversation with Nicodemus (John 3:3), in the eating and drinking of flesh and blood at the Capernaum discourse (chap. 6), and now here in the blood and water issuing from the riven side (cf. I John 5:6-8). No New Testament writer is more certain than John that Christ is now as real and present in the Church and its worship as his earthly life and death were real and present. Christ came; Christ comes; Christ will come: this is John's threefold conviction.

We are familiar with the role of Joseph of Arimathea, "a respected member of the council" (Mark 15:43), in the sepulchral rites; but John tells us that he was assisted by another senator, none other than the learned Nicodemus. The latter's relationship to the disciples was obscure earlier (John 7:50), but it is now quite clear that he has declared himself to be a follower. Perhaps John intended to signify Nicodemus' devotion by the cost of the spices he brought for perfuming the linen winding sheet. The mixture of myrrh and aloes which he brought was enormously heavy.

The Easter Appearance to Mary (20:1-18)

The body of their beloved Master had been placed in a new tomb in a garden near the Skull-place. In the Marcan tradition a group of women including Mary of Magdala went out to the tomb at sunup on Sunday, the first day of the new week. John, however, makes mention of only one, Mary of Magdala, who came to mourn at the grave. She is alarmed to discover the removal of the flat stone which had been pushed up against the entrance to close the rock chamber. When Peter and the beloved disciple learn what has happened, they run from the city to the burial spot to see for themselves. Both Jews and Romans respected burial places and punished severely those who desecrated them.

To an earlier writer, Paul of Tarsus, it was the apostle Peter who first expressed the faith that the crucified Master was alive (I Cor. 15:5). According to John it was not Peter but the beloved disciple who first saw that the tomb was empty and who first believed that the Lord was risen (John 20:5, 8). If John means that the mere sight of the vacant chamber was sufficient to bring the disciple to Easter faith, then his position is not supported by the other evangelists. The women who made the discovery in Mark's account experienced no such joy; they were terrified and sealed their lips about what had happened (Mark 16:8).

But it is the presence of the *risen* Lord confronting them, not the fact of a vacant crypt (which, as Mary first supposes, might mean that the grave had been robbed [John 20:2]) that brings them from grief to joy. *It is the risen Lord who explains the empty sepulchre,* not an empty sepulchre which explains the risen Lord!

Mary has returned to the empty tomb and stands before it in bewilderment overcome with grief. Her solitude is broken by the voice of a man she assumes to be the gardener-caretaker, "Woman, why are you weeping? Whom do you seek?" She pleads that he tell her, if he knows, what has been done with the body of Jesus. It is only when the stranger addresses her by her own name that she recognizes him to be none other than her beloved rabbi (*rabboni*, my Teacher; vs. 16).

Here, in a dramatic scene, is concentrated a basic theme of the Gospel of John and a fundamental insight into the meaning of resurrection faith. For

John's unshakable conviction from first to last is that the Christ of the Church, truly understood, is one and the same as the historical Jesus. The one who meets Mary and the disciples is no stranger arrived from a heavenly court; he bears the marks of a history in which they all have been involved. He is recognized as their beloved Teacher. They can identify him, just as he can call them by name. **Easter faith means recognizing the Jesus of history for the one he truly is, the one who comes from God to bring life to man.** *"That you may believe that Jesus is the Christ, the Son of God, and that believing you·may have life in his name"* (20:31).

The charge given by the Lord to Mary (vs. 17) may suggest the sequence involved in Christ's return to the Father: Resurrection, Ascension, and the arrival of the Holy Spirit. Throughout this Gospel we have been reminded that the coming of Christ from the Father to men in the Incarnation is completed by the return of Christ to God: His death and exaltation, finishing the orbital action, open up the new age of the Church and the Spirit.[16] From the Father—into the world—to the Father—this is the redemptive event that begins a new course of history.

The Easter Appearance to the Disciples (20:19-23)

At first the disciples have only Mary's word that she has seen the Lord. On the evening of the same day, however, the risen Christ suddenly appears in the midst of a group of disciples who are huddled together in an inner room. It is obviously in no merely human form that Christ appears for he passes through closed doors; yet he is visible. Several observations may be made. The Gospel narratives are somewhat vague about the *form* of these Easter appearances, but they are in complete agreement about the *fact* of the appearances. That is to say, the emphasis of these statements is *that* Christ rose from the dead and lives forevermore, not on *how* he makes himself known. Christian experience confirms that. Christ continues to make himself known in different ways to different men perhaps because of varying temperaments and backgrounds. What matters above all else is that we meet him, not when, where, or how we meet him.

Still, we continue to search for some understanding of the form which resurrection life takes. Here Paul comes to our assistance. His interpretation of the spiritual body, related to but distinguished from the natural body, remains the most perceptive and persuasive understanding of the Resurrection (I Cor. 15).

Christ's word of greeting, "Peace" (*shalom*), is followed by a commission. "As the Father sent me, so I send you . . . Receive the Holy Spirit! If you forgive any man's sins, they stand forgiven; if you pronounce them unforgiven, unforgiven they remain" (vss. 21-23, N.E.B.). Again and again throughout this Gospel we hear that Christ comes among men as a heavenly envoy; he is the One-Sent-from-God.[17] In the Intercessory Prayer we heard him identify the work of his disciples with his own mission (17:18; cf. 13:20). They are bound to continue his mission in the world.

In one form after another each of the Gospels concludes with a commission to go and tell. Easter faith meant that or nothing at all. It was not a consoling conviction that they were destined for immortal existence. It meant rather that Jesus and his mission were truly God's word to men and that his disciples were commanded to extend the work begun in Palestine into the whole world. The Christian mission must always be seen as the inescapable consequence of the Easter experience and continuing fellowship with the Lord. Men were not free to amend Christ's work to suit their interests and purposes, choosing what appealed to them, rejecting what did not. It was *his* mission not theirs. Just as he could say, "The Son can do nothing of his own accord, but only what he sees the Father doing," so also the Church must carry on its work in full obedience to the Father's will and Christ's commandments.

The coming of the Holy Spirit to empower and direct that mission, is the risen Lord's gift to the Church. We have been told that Christ's death which is at the same time the moment of his glorification, would be the condition for the coming of the gift of the Spirit (7:39; 16:7). Now we learn what this coming means. As Christ had received authority from the Father to execute judgment and speak the word of forgiveness, so now he confers authority upon the disciples to speak of judgment and forgiveness. This is probably the meaning of the corresponding saying of Jesus in Matthew 16:19; 18:18 and Luke 24:47. High churchmen may read this as a delegation of special authority to a select group, the clergy; but no such restriction is to be found in the text. The disciples, charged with the gospel of judgment and forgiveness, are the representatives of the future Church — the whole community of believers.

This word is both a message to the world and a confirmation of the question of the relationship between believers within the community. Dietrich Bonhoeffer's little book, *Life Together*, is a moving description by a twentieth century martyr of what it means to practice forgiveness within the Christian community. Being Christ's priest to my brother, he observes, means that as a common sinner with him, I can hear his confession and offer forgiveness in Christ's name and that he can do the same for me.

Easter and the Believer (20:24-31)

This passage clearly shows John's concern to interpret the Easter narratives to the Christians of his own day rather than simply to report on the experiences of the first group of eyewitnesses to Jesus' ministry. He begins with the experience of one of the disciples who had been absent at the time of the earlier encounters. Thomas greets with arched eyebrows his friends' reports of a reunion with the risen Lord and the conferral of an authoritative commission through the Holy Spirit. His response is the universal response of those who demand signs and wonders as the basis of their faith. There is something at once ridiculous and sad in the imperious condition he lays down: God must authenticate himself to me on *my* terms. Unless I see and touch, I will not believe. But a sign-based faith, this Gospel teaches, is an undependable and inadequate faith.

It was on the next Sunday, when Thomas and the little company were gathered together in their customary place, that the Lord again made himself known to them (vs. 26). (No doubt John had in mind the fact that Sunday had become the regular day of assembly for Christians in his time, and that men were especially conscious of the Lord's presence when they were in worship.) Thomas now was given the opportunity he craved: tangible proof of the resurrection of his Lord. But it is not said that he seized it. The presence of the Lord is enough to lead him—and us—to a confession which is the crown and climax of the Gospel: "My Lord and my God!" (vs. 28)

What follows has been called the "last and greatest of the beatitudes of the Church." *"Blessed are those who have not seen and yet believe"* (vs. 29; cf. I Pet. 1:8). John hears Christ speaking to the Christians of his own day, separated by hundreds of miles and many years from the primary events of the Crucifixion and Resurrection. Of course the Easter experiences of the first followers of Jesus were

THE LORD OF LIFE AND DEATH

of fundamental importance; the Church was established upon them. But later generations must not make the experiences of the earliest disciples simply objects of veneration and vain longing, or substitutes for their own. Christ is no less vital and real in his Presence among us *now* than he was to those first men and women who believed. Indeed it is these latter-day saints, devoted to him even though they never had the privilege of sharing in the historical events of his ministry, whom Christ addresses as "blessed."

These words permit no disparagement of Christian experience of later times down to our own day. Fellowship with Christ is available to us as it was to them. The Church is not a historical society idolizing the founding fathers, but a continuing company with the fathers which knows and serves the living and present Lord.

John's declaration of purpose (vs. 31) has been before our attention throughout this study. It comes as no surprise discovery at the book's end. Even without this explicit statement, any discerning reader could have surmised the evangelistic intent that led to this presentation of the living Christ. John's urgent concern is that *all* who read and hear may know what it means *to come to life through Christ*. Much more could be told (vs. 30), but enough has been said. The reader is under the challenge of decision.

Afterword:

(I.) The Evangelistic Mission of the Church
(21:1-14)

What follows in chapter 21 is an epilogue to the finished work. Indeed certain linguistic differences and individualities of viewpoint lead many interpreters to conclude that the chapter is the work of another writer, perhaps a leader of the church who edited this book for a wider circulation after the death of the author. What is important, however, is not conjectures about its origin but the message to the Church which is presented here. In the form of an Easter story about a fishing expedition of the disciples, a comparison is drawn between Peter and the beloved disciple and what distinctive contribution each will make in the years ahead. While this seems to be the chief reason for adding the story, there are larger implications to be drawn for the proper tasks of the Church in every age.

The scene is laid by the lake in Galilee with which early tradition identifies some of the resurrection appearances.[18] Peter and six of the disciples seem to have returned to their former occupation of fishing. (Could this have happened *after* the events of chapter 20?) After a full night's work, they are preparing to return to port empty-handed. As they approach shore at daybreak a stranger calls to them from the beach telling them to lower their seine nets once again. When they follow his instructions, the catch is greater than they can haul aboard (vs. 6; cf. Luke 5:1-11). Again it is the unnamed disciple described in terms of endearment who first recognizes the true identity of the stranger. "It is the Lord!" (cf. John 21:7) Peter is the first to *act,* but the beloved disciple is the first to *see* and *understand.*

On shore they share together an early morning meal of bread and fish (vss. 9-13). We noted earlier in our study of the lakeside meal of bread and fish with the multitude that John perceived a connection with the fellowship meal of the Lord's Supper in Christian worship. Here too it is likely that this post-Easter meal of Jesus and his disciples is seen as a symbol of the Lord's Supper in which Christ comes in the Spirit to his own.[19]

The likelihood that this fishing story is intended to convey allegorical meanings increases when we re-examine other features. Why is the specific tally of the catch given? St. Augustine recognized that 153 is the total of the number 17 in arithmetic progression, a number which is the sum of 7 and 10, both of which were often used to signify wholeness and completeness.[20] The story, then, may be a picture of the *world-wide mission of the Church.* Men are to be drawn into fellowship with Christ in the undivided and universal Church until it has reached its complete form. But that mission can only succeed when it is conducted in obedience to the direction of the Church's Lord (21:6) and finds its center in the fellowship of worship. Worship and mission—*coming together* and *going forth; receiving* and *giving*—these are the inseparable double actions of men who have come to life.

Afterword:
(II.) The Teaching Mission of the Church (21:15-25)

The scene which follows similarly seems to convey symbolic teaching about the life and work of the Church. Now the two disciples — Peter and another are at the center of attention. Each has his special tasks to perform which are expressive of the several activities of the Church.

We cannot doubt that the three protests of loyalty by Peter and the three charges of the Lord are set against the three denials by Peter on the night of the arrest. No special distinction of meaning is intended by the slightly different form of the questions and answers (vss. 15-17). In each instance Peter, who is to take a prominent part in the evangelistic mission of the Church, is asked to accept special responsibility as a shepherd (Latin, *pastor*) of the flock of Christ. The shepherd language is familiar. It is Christ himself who is the chief shepherd (10:11, 14; cf. I Pet. 2:25; 5:4); leaders of his community are to be his assistants (cf. Acts 20:28-29; I Pet. 5:2-3). Peter, this writer believed, was the chief figure of missionary and pastoral leadership in the early church, finally meeting martyrdom for the faith (foretold in vs. 18).

Attention turns to the second figure (vss. 20ff.). What is to be the task and the fate of the beloved disciple? In part, the passage is a reply to those who expected that this man and other first generation disciples would survive until the final return of the Lord (cf. Mark 9:1) and were disappointed that it had not happened. This view, the writer contends, is not what the Lord meant by his word about this disciple's lot (vs. 23). This seems to reprove the calculations, speculations, and fussy pryings of adventists into matters outside their proper personal concern.

To the very end this special disciple remains unnamed. But of much greater significance is the function he serves. He is *the one who bears witness* to the whole account of Jesus and his mission and his testimony can be relied upon to be true (vs. 24; cf. 19:35). Peter represents the Church in its missionary and pastoral roles; this man represents the Church in its teaching function. There can be no true life or mission for the Church where the gospel is not really grasped or where Christ is not known to be the revelation of God and his salvation. This is the special contribution of the beloved disciple and it still remains of central importance for the community of faith.[21]

Verse 25 echoes 20:30, reminding the reader that the central figure of the gospel history, Christ, can never be fully explained in any single description or combination of accounts. Against every attempt to weave a web to hold him in a creed, a theology, or a Gospel, it must be reiterated that Christ is greater than anything which can be said about him.

So this Gospel's interpretation of the Life-bringer comes to an end. We are left with a question and an invitation, "Do you love me? Follow me!" The affirmative response is more readily given when the words are heard in the hush of worship, in the seclusion of private devotion, or in the pleasant company of like-minded friends. Can Christ's invitation also be heard in the marketplace, the business office, the laboratory, and the city's alleys? *Christ calls us to follow him* not into the Church but *through the Church into the world* where he continues to carry on his servant ministry (17:15, 18). The Church is the community of those sent out—into that world which is set under God's loving concern—*to proclaim that men everywhere are being called to* **come to life!**

LET YOUR SPIRIT BREAK IN

On your last days on earth
you promised
to leave us the Holy Spirit
as our present comforter.
We also know
that your Holy Spirit blows over this earth.
But we do not understand him.
Many think
he is only wind or a feeling.
Let your Holy Spirit
break into our lives.
Let him come like blood into our veins,
so that we will be driven
entirely by your will.
Let your Spirit
blow over wealthy Europe and America,
so that men there will be humble.
Let him blow over the poor parts of the world,
so that men there need suffer no more.
Let him blow over Africa,
so that men here may understand
what true freedom is.
There are a thousand voices and spirits
in this world,
but we want to hear only your voice,
and be open only to your Spirit.
Amen.

I Lie on My Mat and Pray,
Prayers By Young Africans, ed. by Fritz Pawelzik
(Used by permission of Friendship Press, New York).

Notes

NOTES FOR CHAPTER ONE

[1]Origen of Alexandria, *Against Celsus*, II.27.

[2]Irenaeus, *Against Heresies*, III.11.8.

[3]Clement of Alexandria, according to Eusebius, *History of the Church*, VI.14.7.

[4]Angus J. B. Higgins, *The Historicity of the Fourth Gospel* (London: Lutterworth Press, 1960), p. 64.

[5]Matthew, Mark, and Luke are technically termed the Synoptic Gospels because of the considerable similarities among them in what they tell and how they tell it.

[6]Samuel H. Miller, *The Dilemma of Modern Belief* (New York: Harper & Row, 1963), p. 9.

[7]Albert Camus, *The Rebel*, trans. by Anthony Bower (New York: Vintage Press, 1956), p. 6.

[8]Epiphanius, *Heresies*, LI.2f.

[9]Two early Christian bishops, Papias of Hierapolis and Dionysius of Alexandria, and a document titled *Apostolic Constitutions* testify to such an Ephesian elder named John.

[10]Having paid our respects to literary criticism, hereafter we shall feel free to use the traditional author's name associated with this Gospel without explaining how we would qualify it for the purpose of technical investigation of the problems of origin.

[11]It is worth repeating the words of Martin Luther in his commentary on the Gospel (1.5) as quoted by Alan Richardson, *The Gospel According to Saint John* (London: SCM Press, Ltd., 1959), p. 29

> John speaks as simply and straightforwardly as a child, and his words (as the wise men of the world regard them) sound very childish. But within them there is hidden a majesty so great that no man, however

profound his insight, can fathom or express it.

[12] Papyrus 457, in the John Rylands Library, Manchester, England.

[13] Egerton Pap. 2 in the British Museum, the so-called New Gospel or the British Museum Gospel.

[14] Bodmer Papyrus II and Papyrus XV.

Notes for chapter TWO

[1] The Thanksgiving Hymns from Qumran, while inferior from a literary point of view, are eloquent of a deeply devout spirit. They can be read in an excellent translation by G. Vermès, *The Dead Sea Scrolls in English* (Baltimore: Penguin Books, 1962), Chap. VIII.

[2] Pliny the Younger, *Letters* X.96.

[3] Perhaps vss. 6-8, 12b-13, 17-18.

[4] See the excerpt from *Faust* on page x.

[5] See also Gen. 1:3; Pss. 46:6-7; 147:18; 148:8; etc.

[6] Compare Job 28 and the apocryphal Wisdom of Solomon 7:25; 9:1, 2.

[7] I Cor. 1:24, 30; Col. 2:3; cf. 1:15-17. Though the term Wisdom is not used by the writer of the Letter to the Hebrews, a comparison of Heb. 1:3 with Wisd. of Sol. 7:25-26 shows that the special meaning of the word is known.

[8] See, in the Apocrypha, Wisdom of Sirach 24, especially vss. 3, 23 and cf. 15:1; 19:20; 21:11; 34:8.

[9] Though *logos* is used by John elsewhere in his Gospel (5:24, 38; 8:31, 37, 43, 51-52, 55, etc.), only in the introductory hymn does it have a directly personal sense. Outside of the Gospel, it conveys this sense only in Rev. 19:13 and perhaps I John 1:1 and Heb. 4:12.

[10] A slightly revised form of the N.E.B. text has been divided into the strophic structure such as that prepared by Benjamin W. Bacon, *The Gospel of the Hellenists*, edited by Carl H. Kraeling (New York: Henry Holt & Co., 1933). Bacon italicized verses which he believed represented com-

ments by the editor or redactor. Also see: Joachim Jeremias, *The Central Message of the New Testament* (New York: Charles Scribner's Sons, 1965), p. 74.

[11] William Temple, *Readings in St. John's Gospel* (London Macmillan & Co., Ltd., 1945), p. 5.

[12] This reading of the N.E.B., which combines the latter part of vs. 3 and the first part of vs. 4, is found in the margin of the R.S.V. It is the best attested and preferred form. Note the title for Christ in Acts 3:15, the "Author of life."

[13] Marcion of Pontus, *ca.* A.D. 150, plumped strongly for a division between the realms of creation and redemption, assigning the former to the work of a lesser being called the Demiurge, and the latter to the God revealed by Jesus Christ. Eusebius, *History of the Church* IV.11.

[14] See other passages like Prov. 6:23 and, in the literature between the Testaments, the Wisd. of Sol. 7:26 and the *Test. of Levi* 14:4.

[15] Contrast the saying of the Rabbis: "The Torah is great, because it gives to those who practice it life in this age and in the Age to Come." *Sayings of the Fathers* 6.7.

[16] Here is the first instance of John's use of a word chosen to carry several senses. The verb can be translated "comprehend" or "overcome." Probably John intended both meanings.

[17] In view of the cognate expression found in 6:14; 9:39; 11:27; 12:46; 16:28, the clause here in 1:9 seems to refer not to "every man" but to "the true light"; hence to the fact of the Incarnation.

[18] See, for example, Exod. 4:22-23; Hosea 11:1; Isa. 1:2; 30:1; Jer. 31:9.

[19] On the Tabernacle, see Exod. 24:16; 40:34-38; Num. 14:10. On Wisdom dwelling in Israel, see Sirach 24:8-12; cf. I Enoch. 42:2.

[20] Ps. 8:6. In Isa. 60:1; Hab. 2:14; Rom. 8:18 the glory of God marks the blessed age of the future. For Paul also this transformation into the image of God is already taking place now, II Cor. 3:18.

[21] This ancient reading is now confirmed by both of the important Bodmer third century copies of the Gospel of John.

Notes for Chapter THREE

²²The Greek word used in 1:18 and translated "made known" had the technical meaning in Judaism and Hellenism of an official interpretation of an oracle or a law. Compare Wisdom of Sirach 43:31.

²³Ian T. Ramsey, *Religious Language* (London: SCM, 1957) and William E. Hordern, *Speaking of God* (New York: The Macmillan Co., 1964) are good examples.

²⁴How this affects the communication of the gospel today is challengingly stated in the "Report on the Section on Witness" in *New Delhi Speaks*, ed. by W. A. Visser 't Hooft (New York: Association Press, 1962).

²⁵A phrase from a sermon entitled "The Parable of the Ears" preached by Dr. Dow Kirkpatrick in First Methodist Church, Evanston, Ill., on Oct. 17, 1965.

Notes for Chapter THREE

¹A strange association, since the party of the Pharisees had no authority over the priests. Is this a slip of the pen for Sadducees?

²Deut. 18:15; 34:10. An interesting passage in the *Manual of Discipline* (IX.11), one of the Dead Sea Scrolls, refers to this hope for a new prophet like Moses to arise.

³The *Recognitions* of Clement, I.60, a Jewish-Christian narrative of the third century.

⁴Mark 9:13; Matt. 11:14; 17:12.

⁵It is worth noting that the ram [or lamb] was a symbol of the coming messianic ruler in later Jewish apocalyptic imagery. Early Christian imagery made use of this symbol both in literature and in art. See Acts 8:32; I Pet. 1:19; Rev. 5:6, 12; 14.1, 4.

⁶John says that Bethsaida Julias, to give the full name, was also the home of Andrew and his brother, though Mark locates their home in Capernaum (Mark 1:29).

⁷Some comparative passages will make this clear. See 3:2-3; 4:48; 6:26, 30; 7:31; and compare Matt. 12:38-39; 16:1, 4; Mark 8:11-12; Luke 11:16, 29; 23:8.

⁸He uses an idiom which may be freely translated "Don't

bother me." Examples of its use may be seen in Ezra 4:3; Mark 1:24; 5:7; Matt. 8:29.

[9] Note, for instance, the Bridegroom saying of Mark 2:19-20 and the saying about the Wineskins in Mark 2:22. Cf. also Matt. 22:2-14; Mark 14:24-25. The rabbis themselves often referred to the Torah as comparable to the joy that wine inspires.

[10] Such Jewish writings as the *Assumption of Moses*, the *Psalms of Solomon*, and the Essene *Damascus Rule* are bitter in their protests.

[11] See Ps. 96:8; Isa. 56:7; Ezek. 40 through 48; Mal. 3:1-3 and many passages in the inter-testamental literature.

[12] The Samaritan Temple on Mt. Gerizim had been destroyed in 128 B.C. The magnificent Herodian Temple on Mt. Zion, still under reconstruction in Jesus' day, would be a heap of smoking ashes and rubble by the autumn of A.D. 70, pillaged by the victorious legions of Titus.

[13] It is interesting to note that the Essenes at Qumran spoke of their community as constituting the true Temple of God (*Manual of Discipline*, IX.6). But theirs was a community based on the study and practice of the Torah or Law of Moses. The community of the Resurrection was centered in the new life-in-Christ. See I Cor. 3:9, 16f.; 6:19; Eph. 2:20-22; I Peter 2:5.

[14] This is probably the meaning of the title "ruler of the Jews" in 3:1. See 7:50.

[15] We saw earlier (p. 21) that the word *anōthen* comprehends a double meaning: "again," and "from above."

[16] Ezek. 36:25-27.

[17] The presence of the Spirit would be the distinguishing mark of the Kingdom when it came, the rabbis taught and Scripture affirmed.

[18] This same claim to an exclusive knowledge of the mysteries of the will of God is made in a saying of Jesus in the Synoptic tradition. See Luke 10:22 = Matt. 11:27; and compare Eph. 4:9. The famous Incarnation hymn in Phil. 2:6-11 similarly refers to this "divine parabola" of the humiliation and the exaltation of Christ, showing that this was a very early explanation of the mission of Christ. Cf. Prov. 30:1-4.

Notes for Chapter THREE

[19] Judgment, then, is not the *motive* but the *consequence* of Christ's coming, 3:17; 12:47. It is not a contradiction of this to say that judgment is the corollary of salvation, 5:22-27; 9:39; 12:31. Even so, judgment is primarily the outcome of the decision men make about Christ rather than a sentence imposed by divine fiat. See 3:18; 5:24; 9:39; 12:31; 16:11. The Great Judgment at the end of the world is mentioned only twice: 5:28-29; 12:48.

[20] The word apostle means literally one who is sent. John doesn't actually use this word of Christ but the author of Hebrews does (3:1).

[21] Josephus, *The Antiquities of the Jews*, XVIII.2.2.; XX.6.1.

[22] Jer. 2:13; cf. 17:13; Zech. 14:8; Ezek. 47:9; Isa. 55:1.

[23] See e.g. the Dead Sea Scrolls *Damascus Rule* VIII.6 where the Law is likened to the waters of a well.

[24] Life-giving water is the theme of other passages, such as 3:5; 4:10-15; 7:38; 19:34.

[25] Alternately, we may interpret the passage as a metaphorical allusion to the five earlier deities reverenced by the Samaritan people. Jos. *Antiquities* IX.14.3.

[26] The interval is there (vss. 37-38) but it has been amazingly telescoped. In Jewish teaching and in Jesus' sayings and parables, harvest is a common symbol for the passing away of the present world and the beginning of the new age.

[27] Cf. 6:63, 68; 11:43; 15:3.

[28] *The Methodist Hymnal*, No. 372.

[29] Some interpreters, however, believe this detail may be a misunderstanding of a saying of Jesus about the coming of the Kingdom that is found in Matt. 11:12.

[30] Following the division proposed by Oscar Cullmann in *Early Christian Worship*, trans. by A. Stewart Todd and James B. Torrance (Chicago: Henry Regnery Co., 1953), p. 95.

[31] D. T. Niles, *Reading the Bible Today* (New York: Association Press, Copyright© National Board, Y.M.C.A. 1955), p. 33.

[32] *The Methodist Hymnal*, No. 314.

Notes for chapter FOUR

[1] T. S. Eliot, "The Wasteland," in *Collected Poems, 1909-1935* (London: Faber & Faber, Ltd., 1958), p. 63. See also his "Journey of the Magi" and the musing of Eastern wise men that the real meaning of the birth they came to celebrate was actually a death to the customary life of their kingdoms.

[2] Lev. 23:33-36, 39-43; Deut. 16:13-15; Exod. 23:16.

[3] The Scripture quotation cannot be positively identified. Perhaps Zech. 14:8 comes closest.

[4] This, rather than "no prophet" (R.S.V.), is probably the correct reading as a copy of the Gospel of John in the Bodmer collection now attests.

[5] The tender story of Jesus and the unfaithful betrothed girl, found between these chapters, is an arbitrary intrusion into the text of the Gospel of John from a later time, as the marginal note in the R.S.V indicates. It provides a concrete illustration of Jesus' warning about judgment by appearances in 8:15. Certainly his treatment of the woman is true to the total picture of Jesus in the Gospels; there is no reason to doubt it as a genuine incident, even though it lacked a fixed position in the Gospel tradition.

[6] In the five instances of the affirmation, "I am he" (4:26; 8:24, 28, 58; 13:19), we are probably to recognize an allusion to the well-known statement of Yahweh to Moses "I AM WHO I AM" (Exod. 3:14; *cf.* Isa. 43:10).

[7] An emphasis repeated in 8:51; 14:23-24; 15:20; 17:6 and I John 2:5.

[8] In contemporary terms, that may be to say: If one is Wesley's heir, one will do what Wesley did. Methodist must be reminded that this included an attack on the social evils of his day as well as the more familiar preaching of soul salvation.

[9] In point of fact, the translation in John 9:7 is inaccurate. The word "Siloam" (see Isa. 8:6) really means the "Sender."

[10] H. G. Wells' fantasy, "The Country of the Blind," treats the same theme in an imaginative and powerful way.

[11] Alan Richardson, *The Gospel According to Saint John* (London: SCM Press, Ltd., 1959), p. 127.

Notes for Chapter Four

[12] Beyond this chapter, note the use of the figure in John 21:15-17; Heb. 13:20; I Peter 2:25; 5:4. I am reminded of the little boy who misquoted the Shepherd Psalm and inadvertently stumbled on the Christian's attitude: "The Lord's my shepherd; that's all I want."

[13] Read the famous polemics in Ezek. 34 and Zech. 11:4-17, to name two prominent examples. Some identify the original parable of Jesus in vss. 1-5, to which an interpretation has been added in vss. 7-21.

[14] The eight day festival in December celebrating the rededication of the Temple by Judas Maccabeus on the 25th of Kislev, 165 B.C.

[15] Lev. 24:10-16; Num. 15:30.

[16] The witness of the works is a recurring theme: 5:36; 14:11.

[17] Other examples of the unconscious statement of truth can be found in the jibe of the Pharisees in 12:19 and the title Pilate orders for the cross, 19:19.

[18] Mark 14:3-9 and parallels; Luke 7:36-50; John 12:1-8.

[19] Later tradition identified the woman as Mary of Magdala who subsequently became Mary of Bethany, the disciple of Jesus.

[20] See Ps. 118:25a, 26a.

[21] Previously the hour is not yet come: 2:4; 7:8, 30; 8:20.

[22] Note such passages as 3:19-21; 9:39; 12:37-41; 15:6; 17:2, 6-7; etc.

Notes for Chapter Five

[1] Augustine, *Tractate* LVI.4 "On the Gospel of John."

[2] Cf. Mark 10:45; I Pet. 5:5.

[3] John 19:26f.; 20:2; 21:7, 20.

[4] Jas. 2:8; cf. Gal. 4:6. The injunction to brotherly love was remembered as a key emphasis in the teaching of Jesus. See, for example, Rom. 13:8-10; Gal. 5:13-14; I John 2:7-11; 3:11-23; 4:21; I Tim. 1:5.

[5] H.D.A. Major, T. W. Manson, C. J. Wright, *The Mission*

and Message of Jesus (New York: E. P. Dutton & Co., Inc., 1946), p. 878.

[6]This translation of several possibilities in the Greek is to be preferred to that of the R.S.V.

[7]See also Acts 9:2; 19:9, 23; 22:4.

[8]See also John 1:4, 17.

[9]See also John 1:4; 4:10; 10:10.

[10]See also 15:7, 16; 16:23 and cf. Mark 11:24 and parallels; I John 5:14.

[11]The others are 14:26; 15:26; 16:7; 16:13-15.

[12]1QS [*Manual of Discipline*] III.13-IV.26 Cf. *Test. of Judah* 20:1, 5.

[13]Isa. 40:1; 51:12; 66:13; Luke 2:25; Phil. 2:1.

[14]Acts 4:36; Rom. 12:8; I Cor. 14:3.

[15]Cf. Eph. 2:14-16; 4:3.

[16]Note 12:31; cf. Luke 22:53.

[17]Note how 14:31 seems to bring the discourse to a close.

[18]Ps. 80:8f.; Isa. 5:1-7; Jer. 2:21; Ezek. 15:1-8; 19:10-14; Hosea 10:1f.

[19]The apocryphal *Apocalypse of Baruch* actually speaks of the Messiah as the Vine (*II Bar.* 39:7), perhaps influenced by the messianic title Branch in Zech. 6:12.

[20]Matt. 7:16-20. Vine imagery is frequent in Jesus' teaching recorded in the Synoptic Gospels: Matt. 20:1-16; 21:28-32; Mark 12:1-12; Luke 13:6-9.

[21]In Jewish piety Abraham was named the "friend of God." II Chron. 20:7; Isa. 41:8; Jas. 2:23. With John's usage compare Luke 12:4 and Paul's similar breakthrough in Gal. 4:1-7.

[22]Alan Richardson, *An Introduction to the Theology of the New Testament* (New York: Harper & Bros., 1958), p. 306.

[23]W. A. Visser't Hooft, ed., *New Delhi Speaks* (New York: Association Press, 1962), p. 20.

[24]See 3:19-21; 8:24; 15:22.

[25]See again 12:31; 14:30 and cf. Col. 2:15.

[26]Repeated seven times in this one section!

[27]Knowledge is used in the typically biblical sense of an intimate personal relationship. See, for example, Hosea 4:6; 6:6; Hab. 2:14; Isa. 52:6.

Notes for Chapter SIX

[28] A member of the Woodland Hills Methodist Church in Los Angeles, *Time*, March 11, 1966 (Vol. 87, No. 10), p. 76.

[29] Cf. Eph. 1:10; 4:4-6.

[30] W. H. Auden, "For the Time Being, A Christmas Oratorio," *The Collected Poetry of W. H. Auden* (New York: Random House, 1945), p. 457.

Notes for Chapter SIX

[1] Perhaps a maniple, usually consisting of 200 men, from the *Cohors Secunda Italica* which formed the Roman garrison in Jerusalem.

[2] It must be admitted that it is not clear where the examination takes place: whether in the private home of the high priest or in the Council chambers in the Temple. I am assuming the former alternative. The word translated "court" in verse 15 R.S.V. can refer to a house or the Temple. In any event, it appears to be an informal investigation rather than a trial which takes place.

[3] Cf. John 5:18; 8:59; 10:31; 11:8.

[4] Cf. John 18:33ff.; 19:3, 12, 14f., 19.

[5] It is worth noticing that John's language in verse 13 admits of a double meaning: Pilate sits upon the rostrum or he causes Jesus to sit there. By the latter possibility John suggests who is really the judge and who the judged.

[6] C. K. Barrett, *The Gospel According to St. John* (New York: The Macmillan Co., 1955), p. 445; Paul Winter, *On the Trial of Jesus* (Berlin: Walter de Gruyter & Co., 1951).

[7] No such Paschal custom of amnesty is known to us. Some believe that reference here is made to the power of *indulgentia* sometimes exercised even by provincial officers of lesser rank, but there is not enough evidence to make the case one way or the other.

[8] E.g. *Divi Augusti Filius*, "Son of the deified Augustus."

[9] John identifies it by both Greek and Aramaic names: *Lithōstroton* or Pavement; and *Gabbatha* or raised place.

[10] Recall again that the Synoptists identify the date as

Nisan 15, the first day of the Feast, and the hour of the execution as nine o'clock in the morning (Mark 15:25).

[11] Aramaic, *gulgolthā;* Latin, *calvaria;* "Skull-place," a rocky eminence resembling the shape of a skull.

[12] Cf. Josephus, *Antiq.* III.7.4.

[13] It is the Letter to the Hebrews that develops in greatest detail this interpretation of the death of Christ as a sacrifice.

[14] In *Braggart Warrior.* Plautus was a Roman dramatist of the third century B.C.

[15] *The Roman Way* (New York: W. W. Norton & Co., Inc., 1964), p. 139.

[16] On the exaltation, see 3:13; 6:62; 7:33; 13:1, 3; 14:4, 28; 16:5, 17, 28; 17:13. For the coming of the Spirit see 7:39; 16:7.

[17] Cf. 3:7, 34; 5:36, 38; 6:29, 57; etc.

[18] Matt. 26:32; 28:10, 16-20; and, by implication, Mark 14:28 and 16:7.

[19] In the Roman catacombs of St. Callistus, an early third century symbol of the Lord's Supper appears as a fish bearing a basket containing five round loaves of bread.

[20] Others suggest that the number refers to the ancient view that there were 153 different kinds of fishes.

[21] Apparently this word of endorsement (vs. 24) assumes that the disciple not only bore witness but that he himself wrote this Gospel. We have suggested reasons why this early explanation of the writing of the Gospel may be mistaken.

Glossary

ABBREVIATIONS:

A.D.—(Latin: *anno Domini*)—In the year of our Lord.

A.R.V.—American Standard Revised Version of the Bible.

B.C.—Before Christ.

ca.—(Latin: *circa*)—*about.*

cf.—compare.

f.—following (verse or page); ff.—following (verses or pages).

i.e.—(Latin: *id est*)—that is.

ibid.—the same reference.

K.J.V.—King James Version of the Bible.

N.E.B.—New English Bible.

p.—page; pp.—pages.

par.—parallel.

R.S.V.—Revised Standard Version of the Bible.

viz.—(Latin: *videlicet*)—namely.

vs.—verse; vss.—verses.

ADVENTIST—a believer in the doctrine of Adventism (the doctrine that the second coming of Christ and the end of the world are at hand).

ADVOCATE—a counselor, lawyer or one who pleads the cause of another.

ALLEGORY—a symbolic narrative or illustrative story.

ANALOGY—a comparison between two similiar things; or between two things having some relation to each other; resemblances or agreements between different terms or things under comparison.

APOCALYPSE—a revelation, a prophetic disclosure or announcement of the ultimate reign of God; specifically, the Revelation of St. John.

APOCALYPTIST—a writer or exponent of apocalyptic writings (books of revelations based on dreams or visions); chiefly used to refer to Jewish and early Christian prophets who predicted in visionary terms the glorious coming of the Messiah and the speedy establishment of the Kingdom of God.

APOCRYPHAL—literally, "hidden" or "stored away", referring to a group of fourteen Jewish writings from the 2nd century B.C. through the first century A.D., not regarded of canonical worth by Judaism and Protestanism; they are accepted by Roman Catholics, Eastern Orthodox, Anglicans, and some others.

APOSTATE—a term designating a believer who has renounced his faith, belief, party, or church and withdrawn from the religious community.

APOSTROPHE—a digression, especially in the form of personal address to someone who is usually not present.

AUTHENTICATE—to establish as genuine.

CANON—the books of the Bible; the collection or list of books accepted by the Christian Church as genuine and inspired by the Holy Spirit.

CATACOMB—an underground gallery or passage with recesses for tombs.

CATEGORY—a general term designating a class or group to which several specific terms may belong.

CLEMENT OF ALEXANDRIA (A.D. 150-215)—a Greek theologian of the early church, probably born at Athens, who studied at Alexandria; regarded as the founder of the Alexandrian school of theology. In his eight volume work entitled *Outlines,* he summarized the scriptural books and reported the tradition of the Church regarding the composition and order of the Gospels.

COGNATE—that which is related by common stock or origin; allied in nature or quality.

COLLOCATION—act of placing side by side in a definite order; to arrange; also, such a close arrangement.

CONGENITAL—a condition existing before or from birth; constitutional.

CONNOTATION—the suggestive significance of a word apart from its essential and recognized meaning.

COSMIC—characteristic of the cosmos, hence vast, immeasurably extended in time and space.

CRESCENDO—a gradual increase in volume of sound or emphasis.

CRITERION—a standard of judging; a rule or test by which a thing is tried.

CRYPTIC—hidden; secret.

CULPABILITY—guilt.

DEAD SEA SCROLLS—a library of almost six hundred biblical and Jewish sectarian writings, dating from the second century B.C. to the first century A.D.; discovered in 1947 in caves above the northwestern shores of the Dead Sea.

DEMIURGE—in certain Gnostic religious systems, a divine being — subordinate to the supreme deity

GLOSSARY

— who was held to be the creator of the universe.

DESECRATED—violated; profaned, especially something sacred.

DISPERSION—Jewish families scattered through the countries of the ancient world outside Palestine from the time of the Babylonian exile in the sixth century B.C. through the Greek and Roman periods. In Jesus' day approximately four million Jews lived in the Roman empire in contrast to a half million settled in the homeland.

EBIONITES—a Jewish-Christian sect of the second century, with centers in Alexandria and Syria, which regarded Christ as the final prophet and held that the Law as well as faith was essential to salvation.

ENIGMATIC—puzzling; mysterious.

EPHEMERAL—transitory; short-lived.

ESSENES—a Jewish sect originating in the second century B.C. which established monastic and non-monastic communities, such as the settlement at Qumran described in the Dead Sea Scrolls.

EXISTENTIALISM—a contemporary philosophical position, assuming both atheistic and theistic forms, which emphasizes the involvement of the total self, not just the intellect, in an undertanding of individual human existence and in the search to become a real person.

EXPERTISE—highly specialized technical skill or language.

FACTIONALISM—party strife or partisan activity by a small group within a larger group—often from limited or selfish motives.

FEAST OF TABERNACLES (SUKKOTH)—a popular seven or eight day Jewish festival celebrated in September-October and commemorating the march through the Sinai wilderness by the Hebrew fugitives from Egypt.

GAIUS (A.D. 160-230)—a Roman church leader and anti-Montanist who doubted the authorship of the Fourth Gospel.

GNOSTIC—a member of a sect claiming special knowledge of spiritual things.

GNOSTICISM—a philosophical and religious movement—including some sects of early Christians —whose adherents claimed to have superior knowledge of spiritual things, obtained through direct insight, and who held that the world was created by powers or agencies arising as emanations from the Godhead.

HALLEL PSALM—the Hallel is a group of Psalms (113-118) sung in connection with several important Jewish festivals, especially Passover.

HANUKKAH—the eight-day festival of lights observed by Jewish families to commemorate the victory of the Maccabees over Antiochus of Syria and the rededication of the defiled temple in Jerusalem.

HELLENISM—the composite culture, predominately Greek, of the Mediterranean world from the time of Alexander the Great through the later years of the Roman Empire, roughly 300 B.C. to A.D. 300.

HERACLITUS (530-470 B.C.)—Greek philosopher, born at Ephesus of distinguished parentage. From his lonely life, the extreme profundity and obscurity of his philosophy and his contempt for mankind, he was called the "Dark Philosopher." He taught that cosmic history is subject to a law *(logos)* of change in continuous cycles which begin and end in fire.

INALIENABLE—inseparable, incapable of being alienated, surrendered, or transferred.

INCOGNITO—with one's identity hidden, as under another name.

INQUISITORS—those who ask questions; especially referring to the inquirers or examiners of the Inquisition.

INSCRUTABLE—unfathomable; not understandable.

INTERMEDIARY—a go-between.

INTER-TESTAMENTAL—between the Old and New Testaments.

IRENAEUS (A.D. 130-200)—Bishop of Lyons who wrote a number of important works, chief among which was one called *Heresies Answered*.

JURIDICAL—that which pertains to the administration of law and justice or the office of a judge.

LITURGIST—one who favors or adheres to a liturgy (public service, divine worship). Also an expert in liturgical history of custom.

LOGOS—Divine Word; the actively expressed, creative, and revelatory thought and will of God, recognized as identical with God, and at the same time distinguished from God; identified in the Fourth Gospel (John 1:1-18) with Jesus Christ.

LULABS—festive palm branches carried at the Feast of Tabernacles.

LUSTRATION—ceremony for purification by propitiatory offering or other ceremonial, such as washing, ablution.

MANIPLE—a unit of the Roman army consisting of 60 or 120 soldiers.

MENDELIAN LAW—pertaining to a principle of heredity, formulated by G. J. Mendel (1822-84), which

GLOSSARY

describes the inheritance of distinctive characteristics in animals and plants.

MESSIANIC—of or pertaining to the Messiah; especially, the "messianic hope" or "age."

METAPHOR—a figure of speech: as, "the ship *plows* the sea;" metaphors seem to identify while similes merely compare.

METAPHYSICAL—that division of philosophy which includes the study of being, ontology; and the science of the fundamental causes and processes of things, cosmology.

MONOTHEISM—the doctrine that there is but one God.

MONTANISTS—a second century Christian sect in Asia Minor which stressed the gift of ecstatic prophecy through the Holy Spirit and the imminent coming of Christ.

MONTANUS (ca. A.D. 160)—the leader of a Christian heretical sect centering in Phrygia in Asia Minor who proclaimed himself as the special instrument of the Holy Spirit in ecstatic prophesying of the coming of the New Jerusalem in Phrygia.

MYSTERY CULT—secret religious societies, widely popular throughout the Roman Empire in New Testament times, which featured highly emotional rituals to secure personal salvation or an improved status in the life to come.

OBVERSE—the opposite of reverse.

OSTRACISM—temporary exclusion by general consent from common privileges, favor, etc.

PARABLE—a story, allegory, or comparison with a purpose told in terms to cause the hearer to compare and assess his own actions.

PARABOLIC—of the nature of a parable; allegorical.

PARACLETE—Holy Spirit, Comforter (K.J.V.); Counselor (N.E.B.); English spelling of the distinctive Greek word for the Spirit of God, in the Gospel of John.

PAROCHIAL—or pertaining to a parish; often implying narrow or limited interests or opinions.

PASCHAL SACRIFICE—in Jewish terms, the lamb that was slain and roasted for the Passover supper. In Christian terms, the death of Jesus (see I Cor. 5:7).

PASSION OF JESUS—the gospel story of the final sufferings of Christ from the Last Supper to his death on the cross.

PATRIMONY—estate inherited from one's father or other ancestor.

PENTECOST—a solemn festival of the Jews, celebrated on the fiftieth day after the seventh day of the Passover; a Christian festival commemorating on the seventh Sunday after Easter the descent of the Holy Spirit upon the Apostles.

PENTECOSTALISTS—the name applied to several sects of believers, originating in America in 1906, who stress the importance of baptism by the Holy Spirit which manifests itself in speaking in tongues and in divine healing.

PHILO—Philo Judaeus, or Philo of Alexandria, also known as "the Jewish Plato"; sought, ca. 1 A.D. to harmonize the philosophies and religions of Plato, Aristotle, and others with the doctrines of the Pentateuch.

PLATO—Greek philosopher, born ca. 428 B.C., died ca. 348 B.C. About 387 B.C., he founded the Academy for the systematic pursuit of philosophical and scientific research; but he is primarily important to us as one of the greatest philosophical writers. He taught that the tangible world is an imperfect expression of a real world of Ideas or Forms subordinated to the Idea of the good.

POST-EXILIC—after the exile; specifically, the period in Jewish history following the Babylonian captivity which continued from 597 to ca. 527 B.C. Therefore, after 527 B.C.

PREDESTINARIAN—referring to a theological view which holds that the course of human life is determined by God before it comes to pass.

PRIMORDIAL—first created or existing; rudimentary, as *primordial matter*.

PROSELYTE—a new convert, especially to some religious sect, or to some opinion, system, or party.

SANHEDRIN—the high court of the Jewish state during the early Roman period which met in the Temple at Jerusalem and consisted of 71 representatives of the priestly class and principal religious parties.

SCHISM—a division or split in a religious body resulting in groups maintaining separate existence.

SEDER—the religious service and ritual supper commemorating the deliverance of the Jews from Egypt; it marks the opening night of the FEAST OF PASSOVER.

SEMANTIC—pertaining to the development and range of meanings expressed in words.

SEMINAL—containing seed; source, or first principle; germinal; originative.

SHALOM—Hebrew word for peace.

SON OF MAN—a mysterious heavenly being in Jewish apocalyptic thought, identified by the author of John's Gospel with Jesus as the mediator between God and man.

SOPHIA-LOGOS—Greek words for wisdom and word respectively; in

GLOSSARY

occult Judaism signifying either the heavenly Torah or the deity; in some phases of early Christian thought applied to the risen and reigning Christ (see LOGOS).

STOIC—one who believes that wise men should be free from all passion, unmoved by either joy or grief, submissive to natural law.

STROPHE—a separate section in a poem which, unlike a stanza, does not follow a metrical pattern.

SUKKOTH—see FEAST OF TABERNACLES.

SUPERNAL—being in or coming from heaven or belonging to a realm above and beyond this world.

SYNOPTIC—affording a synopsis, or general view, of a whole; the first three Gospels, which are more or less parallel.

TABERNACLED—placed in a temple; literally, "tented;" i.e., lived or slept in a tent.

TATIAN (ca. A.D. 170)—a Syrian Christian leader who prepared a composite form of the Four Gospels called the *Diatessaron;* in his later years he became the leader of a heretical sect.

THEMATIC—relating to a theme; a subject or discourse; a text.

THEATRE OF THE ABSURD—moves toward a radical devaluation of language and toward the emergence of a poetry based on concrete images springing out of theatrical action.

THEOSOPHY—Philosophical or religious thought in which a claim is made to special insight into the nature of God, arrived at neither by external historic fact, nor by scientific induction, but by direct perception independent of any reasoning process. Today the term is usually understood to refer to a movement begun in 1875 to promote universal brotherhood on the basis of "the ancient wisdom," chiefly Hindu or by a combination of both; often identified with the "ancient wisdom" of India.

TORAH—a Hebrew word for "teaching" which was applied to the revelation embodied in the law of Moses comprising the first five books of the Old Testament and more precisely defined in terms of the 613 commandments identified therein.

UNITARY—pertaining to that which is whole and undivided.

VALEDICTORY—a bidding farewell; address of farewell.

VICARIOUS—acting in place of, or in behalf of, another; here the suffering and death of Christ as a substitute for guilty men.

YAHWEH—the distinctive name of God in the Old Testament, translated "the Lord" in K.J.V. and R.S.V.

Books Suggested for Further Reading on the *Gospel of John*

Your local church, public or college library may be able to lend out-of-print books to you.

APPLETON, GEORGE. *John's Witness to Jesus.* World Christian Books. New York: Association Press, 1955. (Out-of-print.)

BARCLAY, WILLIAM. *The Gospel of John.* The Daily Study Bible Series, 2nd ed. Philadelphia: Westminster Press, 1958. 2 vol.

BERKELEY, J. P. *Reading the Gospel of John.* Valley Forge, Pa. The Judson Press, 1966.

BROWN, RAYMOND E. *The Gospel According to John.* The Anchor Bible 29, Vol. I, chs. 1-12. New York: Doubleday, 1966.

CRANNY, T. F. *John 17: As We Are One.* Garrison, N.Y.: Graymoor, 1966.

ERDMAN, C. R. *The Gospel of John*, Philadelphia: Westminster Press, 1966 (reprint).

EVANS, O. E. *The Gospel According to St. John*. Naperville, Ill.: Alec R. Allenson, Inc., 1965.

FILSON, FLOYD V. *John*. Richmond, Va.: John Knox Press, 1963.

GRANT, FREDERICK C. *The Gospel of John in the King James Version*. Harper's Annotated Bible Series. New York: Harper & Row, 1957. 2 vol. (Out-of-print.)

GUY, HAROLD A. *The Gospel and Letters of John*. New York: St. Martin's Press, 1963.

HAMILTON, WILLIAM. *The Modern Reader's Guide to John*. Reflection Books. New York: Association Press, 1959.

HOSKYNS, E. C. and DAVEY, F. N. *The Fourth Gospel*, 2nd rev. ed. Naperville, Ill.: Alec R. Allenson, Inc., 1956.

HOWARD, WILBERT F. and GOSSIP, ARTHUR JOHN. "The Gospel According to St. John." *The Interpreter's Bible*, Vol 8. Nashville: Abingdon Press, 1952.

HUNTER, A. M. *The Gospel According to John*. The Cambridge Bible Commentary: New English Bible. Cambridge, England: Cambridge University Press, 1965.

LIGHTFOOT, ROBERT H. *St. John's Gospel*: *A Commentary*, ed. C. F. Evans. Oxford: Clarendon Press, 1956.

MAJOR, H. D. A., MANSON, T. W., and WRIGHT, C. J. *The Mission and Message of Jesus*: An Exposition of the Gospels in the Light of Modern Research. New York: E. P. Dutton, 1938.

MARSH, JOHN. *The Gospel According to St. John*. Baltimore: Penguin Books, 1968.

MUSSNER, FRANZ. *The Historical Jesus in the Gospel of St. John*, trans. by W. J. O'Hara. New York: Herder & Herder, 1967.

RICHARDSON, ALAN. *The Gospel According to St. John*. Torch Bible Commentaries. New York: The Macmillan Co., 1962.

SANDERS, J. N. *A Commentary on the Gospel According to St. John*, ed. B. A. Mastin. New York: Harper & Row, 1969.

SMART, W. A. *The Spiritual Gospel*. Nashville: Abingdon-Cokesbury Press, 1946. (Out-of-print.)

TEMPLE, WILLIAM. *Readings in St. John's Gospel*. New York: St. Martin's Press, 1945.

TITUS, ERIC L. *The Message of the Fourth Gospel*. Nashville: Abingdon Press, 1957. (Out-of-print.)

WESTCOTT, B. F. and FOX, ADAM. *The Gospel According to St. John*. London: James Clarke & Co., 1958.

The Author

DR. ERNEST W. SAUNDERS is Dean of the Seminary and Professor of New Testament Interpretation at Garrett Theological Seminary, Evanston, Illinois.

Dr. Saunders was born in Boston, Massachusetts. After studying three years at Northeastern University, majoring in Chemical Engineering, he entered Boston University, receiving there the B.S. degree in Religious Education from the School of Religious and Social work. In 1940 he graduated from the School of Theology, *magna cum laude*, with the degree of S.T.B.

His graduate study was done at Duke University, from which he received the Ph.D. degree in Biblical Studies, and the University of Basle.

Dr. Saunders is married to Verina May Rogers who holds A.B. and M.A. degrees in Religious Education from Boston University. They have three children: Leslie Ann, Duncan Reid, and Charles Spencer.

Dr. Saunders' publications include: *Jesus in the Gospels* (Prentice-Hall, 1967) articles in *The Interpreter's Dictionary of the Bible* (1962); *Biblisch-Historisches Handwoerterbuch* (1963); and *Westminster Dictionary of Christian Education.*